DISCIPLESHIP|EXPLORED

WHAT'S THE BEST LOVE YOU'VE EVER KNOWN?

LEADER'S HANDBOOK

Discipleship Explored Leader's Handbook (3rd Edition)
Copyright © 2018 Christianity Explored.
Reprinted 2018, 2019, 2022.
www.explo.red

Published by:
The Good Book Company

thegoodbook.com | www.thegoodbook.co.uk
thegoodbook.com.au | thegoodbook.co.nz | thegoodbook.co.in

CHRISTIANITY
EXPLORED
MINISTRIES

ISBN: 9781784982034 | Printed in Turkey

Design by André Parker

WELCOME TO
DISCIPLESHIP|EXPLORED

The last recorded words of Jesus – "Go and make disciples" – ought to be the first priority of his followers. But how do we make disciples?

As a student, my experience of being discipled was pretty straightforward. Every week or so, a kind and persistent friend would make me a cup of tea. Then we'd look at a short section of Scripture together to see what it said about God, what it said about us, and what we should do as a result. Then he'd ask me if there was any way he could be praying for me. Occasionally, if it was a good week, I'd be offered a cookie. It was completely unassuming, and utterly life-changing.

My hope for *Discipleship Explored* is that it would equip you to do just what that friend did for me. I want to reassure you that you don't need to have years of teaching experience. All you need is the prayerful desire to explore Paul's letter to the Philippians alongside another believer or group of believers.

And here's the best part. The pressure is taken off you because the focus isn't on you. The focus is on Jesus Christ, and thankfully he is a great deal more magnetic, more persuasive, and more powerful than any of us.

So let's open up Philippians with a sense of wonder, joy, and expectation. Paul is about to show us the greatest love we've ever known.

Barry Cooper

CONTENTS

SECTION 1
HOW TO RUN
DISCIPLESHIP EXPLORED

discipleship.explo.red
is the official website for *Discipleship Explored*, featuring content for both guests and leaders.

Registering your course is free, and gives you access to even more content. You'll also be able to watch the films online and share them with others.

GETTING
STARTED

What's the aim of *Discipleship Explored*?

The key phrase of Philippians is "in Christ."

So the aim of *Discipleship Explored* is to thrill followers of Jesus with the confidence, unity, righteousness, and love which are theirs "in Christ."

Who's it for?

Discipleship Explored is designed to be enjoyed by all followers of Christ, whether veteran or just starting out. You can run it one to one or in larger groups.

What's the structure of *Discipleship Explored*?

Discipleship Explored has eight sessions, each one exploring a short section of Philippians. The main components are simple:

- **Film** | 15 minutes
- **Explore Philippians** | 45 minutes

Between each session, there are Follow Up Bible readings for guests to explore at home. They're designed to help believers establish a rhythm of daily Scripture-reading, memorization, and prayer.

	⊙ Film	☰ Discussion	↱ Follow Up
Session 1 **Confident in Christ**	Confident in Christ	Philippians 1:1-11	Assurance: Ephesians 2:8-10 John 10:27-28
Session 2 **Living in Christ**	Living in Christ	Philippians 1:12-26	The Holy Spirit: Ephesians 1:13-14 Galatians 5:16-23
Session 3 **One in Christ**	One in Christ	Philippians 1:27 – 2:11	Meeting Together: Colossians 3:12-17 1 Peter 2:9-12
Session 4 **Obedient in Christ**	Obedient in Christ	Philippians 2:12-30	Scripture: 2 Timothy 3:14-17 Psalm 19:7-8

	△ Film	☰ Discussion	↗ Follow Up
Session 5 **Righteous in Christ**	Righteous in Christ	Philippians 3:1-9	Righteousness: Romans 3:20-24 Romans 5:6-10
Session 6 **Transformed in Christ**	Transformed in Christ	Philippians 3:10-21	Pressing On: Matthew 6:19-24 Matthew 7:24-27
Session 7 **Rejoicing in Christ**	Rejoicing in Christ	Philippians 4:1-9	Prayer: Matthew 6:5-13 Colossians 1:3-14
Session 8 **Content in Christ**	Content in Christ	Philippians 4:10-23	Contentment: 1 Timothy 6:6-12 Colossians 3:1-10

How long does each session last?

Discipleship Explored is as flexible as you are. You can cover each session in an hour if time is at a premium. The session will take a little longer if you prefer to meet beforehand for a meal or coffee.

What's the aim of each film?

The films are designed to unpack the meaning of Philippians and to help believers apply it. They're written and presented by Barry Cooper, and feature interview footage from believers all over the world.

How should I start each session?

If possible, invite your guest(s) to arrive about 30 minutes before the session officially starts. That gives you time to share food or coffee first so you can relax and get to know each other better. It also helps you start and finish your session on time.

Hospitality is one of the ways the Philippian church "work out [their] salvation" (Philippians 2:12), so this is a great way to put Philippians into practice.

How should I end each session?

At the end of each session, thank your guest(s) for coming, and make it clear that they're very welcome to stay around if they'd like. Some of the best conversations will happen over a cup of coffee once the session has ended.

What's the best way to prepare for *Discipleship Explored*?

☐   Pray! And keep praying throughout the series.

☐   Read Philippians several times.

☐ Get to know your fellow leaders, if you have any. A major theme of Philippians is unity (the Greek word *koinonia*) between believers, so it's good for guests to experience that firsthand.

☐ Read through the discussion questions and answers in this Leader's Handbook.

☐ Watch the short films so you know what to expect.

☐ Familiarize yourself with the "Questions About Philippians" section on page 115.

☐ Prepare yourself for the "big seven" tough questions on page 39.

☐ Be ready to share briefly with guests how you became a follower of Jesus (1 Peter 3:15).

☐ See "How do I encourage people to come?" in the FAQs on page 37.

☐ Register your course at **www.discipleship.explo.red/register** That will give you access to additional resources for leaders and guests.

Why Philippians?

Discipleship Explored isn't a systematic look at all the individual elements that are involved in discipleship, though you will find material here on reading the Bible, being committed to the local church, prayer, evangelism, serving others, and so on. Instead, we look at one short letter in which Paul's main focus is Christ and his "surpassing worth" (Philippians 3:8). This is by design.

My pastor, Larry Kirk, tells the story of two dancers. The first puts her earbuds in, hits "play," and, because she hears the music she loves best in all the world, she starts to dance with rhythm and energy and grace and joy. She's captivated and enthralled by the music.

The second dancer looks at the first, doesn't see the earbuds, and thinks, "That looks fun!" And though she can't hear any music herself, she tries to copy the moves anyway.

It works for a time, sort of. But because she can't hear the music, her movement is clunky, hesitant, and self-conscious. She doesn't seem to enjoy dancing the way the first dancer does. And before too long, she's running out of energy.

Some books and resources on discipleship can put you in the position of that second dancer. They encourage you to learn all the right moves – read your Bible, pray, go to church – but without enabling you to hear the music that drives it all.

The aim of *Discipleship Explored* is to "turn up the music." What we really need, if we're to be disciples of Jesus, aren't clever techniques or lists of things to do. Lots of people know all the right moves, but never become genuine disciples.

What we need, first and foremost, is what the Philippians needed. We need our hearts to be captivated and enthralled by the surpassing worth of Christ.

ABOUT
PHILIPPIANS

Who wrote it?

The apostle Paul wrote the letter to the Philippians. Not only does Paul identify himself as the author within the letter, but Paul's writing style is much in evidence, and the early church unanimously believed it to be his work.

Where was it written?

Philippians 1:13-14 tells us that Paul wrote the letter while "in chains." Most likely, this was the period of his life when he was under house arrest in Rome (Acts 28:14-31). Paul was allowed to live by himself in his own rented house, albeit with a soldier to guard him. He was also free to receive visitors, teaching them about the Lord Jesus Christ "with all boldness and without hindrance!"

When was it written?

The evidence suggests that it was written around AD 61.

Who was he writing to?

Followers of Christ in Philippi, Macedonia (in modern-day Greece). The city of Philippi was a bustling Roman colony whose inhabitants prided themselves on being Roman citizens. Many Philippians made a point of speaking Latin, and even dressed like Romans. This is perhaps why Paul makes a point of stressing, "But our citizenship is in heaven" (Philippians 3:20).

Why was it written?

First and foremost, Paul wrote because he dearly loved the believers in Philippi, perhaps more fondly than any of the other believers he addressed in his New Testament letters. He says, "God can testify how I long for all of you with the affection of Christ Jesus" (Philippians 1:8).

But Paul also wanted to thank the Philippians for the gift they'd sent via their messenger Epaphroditus, when they found out Paul had been detained (Philippians 4:10, 18).

As he writes, Paul reports on his present circumstances, encourages them to stand firm and rejoice in the face of persecution, urges them to be humble and united, warns them against certain dangerous teachers, and reminds them of the righteousness that is theirs in Christ.

What's distinctive about the letter?

It's been called the New Testament letter of joy. The word "joy," in its various forms, occurs sixteen times in Philippians.

It's also the letter of *koinonia*, a Greek word meaning partnership or oneness. See for example Philippians 1:4-5, where Paul writes, "In all my prayers for all of you, I always pray with joy, because of your partnership (*koinonia*) in the gospel from the first day until now…"

Koinonia is a word that stresses how communal the Christian life must be. If someone were to say to Paul that they loved Jesus, but weren't committed to their local church, Paul would have had little confidence that they were followers of Jesus at all.

The word is also used to describe our union with Christ as believers: "Therefore if you have any encouragement from being united with Christ, if any comfort from his love, if any common sharing (*koinonia*) in the Spirit…" (Philippians 2:1).

For Paul, *koinonia* with Christ leads to *koinonia* with other believers.

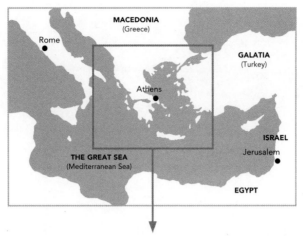

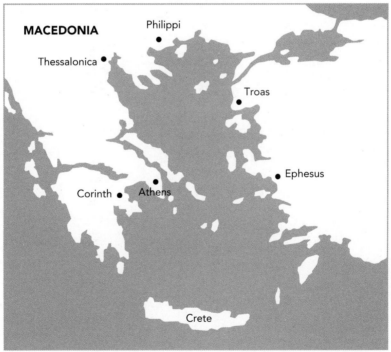

This map is included on page 79 of the guest Handbook.

BEING A
DISCIPLESHIP EXPLORED
LEADER

Read 2 Timothy, chapters 1 and 2

What happened after Philippians was written? How did the story continue? This letter from Paul to Timothy gives us a valuable insight – and suggests the way Paul might speak to us as we prepare to lead *Discipleship Explored*.

Timothy was the young evangelist who had accompanied Paul on his first visit to Philippi. Paul thought of him with great fondness, even calling him "my dear son" (2 Timothy 1:2).

Paul wrote the letter around AD 67, shackled in a Roman prison and aware that he was going to die soon. Many followers of Christ had deserted him (2 Timothy 1:15), so his urgent appeal to Timothy was to guard, protect, and pass on the truth about Jesus Christ.

As Paul does so, he warns Timothy that doing this won't be easy. He likens it to the life of a soldier, for whom risk and suffering are a matter of course:

"You then, my son, be strong in the grace that is in Christ Jesus. And the things you have heard me say in the presence of many witnesses entrust to reliable people who will also be qualified to teach others. Join with me in suffering, like a good soldier of Christ Jesus. No one serving as a soldier gets entangled in civilian affairs, but rather tries to please his commanding officer." (2 Timothy 2:1-4)

Commenting on verse 4, the early Christian writer Tertullian says, "No soldier goes to war equipped with luxuries, nor does he go forth to the battle-line from his bed-chamber, but from light and narrow tents wherein every hardship and roughness and uncomfortableness is to be found."

Being a *Discipleship Explored* leader doesn't mean you have to live in a tent for the duration of the series – but it will mean the soldier's life: discipline, responsibility, and commitment.

In particular, we'll need to be committed in three ways:

1. Committed to prayer

Paul opens his letter to Timothy by saying, "Night and day I constantly remember you in my prayers" (2 Timothy 1:3). Because we realize that no spiritual growth can happen without God's enabling, we too need to be constantly remembering our guests and fellow leaders in prayer.

2. Committed to Scripture

We must be convinced, with Paul, that God's word is where the power is. Whatever his personal circumstances, Paul knew that if the word were preached, it would do its work: "I am suffering even to the point of being chained like a criminal. But God's word is not chained" (2 Timothy 2:9).

As a result, Paul exhorts Timothy – and every Christian teacher – to devote himself to the study of God's word: "Do your best to present yourself to God as one approved, a workman who does not need to be ashamed and who correctly handles the word of truth" (2 Timothy 2:15).

In getting ready for *Discipleship Explored*, it's vital that you immerse yourself in Philippians. If the message of Philippians doesn't excite you, it won't be exciting for a guest. And if it hasn't begun to transform your character, it's unlikely to start transforming those who are following your lead.

3. Committed to people

The way we love our guests will be one of the most lasting and persuasive things we'll say about the Lord Jesus during *Discipleship Explored*. We are not the gospel (Jesus is), but our lives should make the teaching about our Savior attractive.

We must be willing to open up our own lives for inspection, and talk about our own weaknesses and failures, as well as the ways that Christ has changed us. Such genuine love and honesty are the marks of a true disciple of Christ, and in and of themselves they can be a compelling answer to many of the doubts people may have.

Being committed in these three ways will require us to be single-minded. As 2 Timothy 2:4 says, "No one serving as a soldier gets entangled in civilian affairs, but rather tries to please his commanding officer."

Often, as we seek to make time to pray, study Philippians, and meet with group members, the good will be the enemy of the best, and the urgent will be the enemy of the important. We may find temptations or feelings of inadequacy creeping in. Sometimes, leading will be a real struggle: physically, emotionally, and spiritually. After all, our enemy, Satan, hates the work we are doing.

But we keep going, for the joy of pleasing our "commanding officer," the Lord Jesus Christ. And we "endure everything for the sake of the elect, that they too may obtain the salvation that is in Christ Jesus, with eternal glory" (2 Timothy 2:10).

BEFORE
DISCIPLESHIP EXPLORED

Get to know Philippians, the Handbook and the films

- Read through Philippians a few times.
- Familiarize yourself with the questions and the answers in Section 2 of this Leader's Handbook (page 47).
- Watch each film before you run the session so you're familiar with it.

Get to know your fellow leader(s) if you have any

It's important that guests see as well as hear what it means to live as a follower of Jesus Christ. So a good relationship with your co-leader(s) is essential. Get to know each other, and pray with each other before and during the series.

Prepare your personal story

"Always be prepared to give an answer to everyone who asks you to give the reason for the hope that you have. But do this with gentleness and respect..." (1 Peter 3:15)

At some point, there may well be an opportunity to share your story with the group – or someone will ask how you became a follower of Jesus yourself. Often, guests will ask you about your experience of living as a disciple of Jesus.

As far as possible, keep the focus on who Christ is, what he has done, and what he means to you. Notice how in Philippians 3:4-14, Paul's description of his own background only takes up three verses – the rest is all about the "surpassing worth" of Christ.

Prepare for difficult questions

Discipleship Explored is an ideal place for people to ask questions. The Appendices, starting on page 107, will help you prepare for some of the most common questions that people ask about Christianity in general, and Philippians in particular.

Pray

- that those invited will come.
- that God will enable you to prepare well and lead faithfully.
- for deepening friendships with your co-leaders and guests.
- that the Spirit will open people's eyes to the beauty of Jesus Christ.
- that you and your guests will be empowered by the Spirit to live as Philippians calls us to live.

Anticipate pastoral issues

Try to anticipate the pastoral issues that will be particularly relevant to the guest(s) in your care, and make a note of Scripture (especially Philippians), Christian books, or articles that might be helpful to them. The list below doesn't cover every possible issue, but may be a helpful starting point.

How would you help a person who is...

- unsure that God can forgive them for something they've done? (Philippians 1:4-6; Hebrews 4:15-16; 1 John 1:8-9)

- sleeping with a partner outside marriage? (Philippians 1:27a; 1 Corinthians 7:2; Ephesians 5:3; 1 Thessalonians 4:3)

- dealing with addictions? (Philippians 3:1; 1 Corinthians 6:12; Titus 2:11-12)

- coping with broken family relationships? (Philippians 3:20; Matthew 19:27-29)

- dating a non-Christian girlfriend or boyfriend? (Philippians 2:1-2; 2 Corinthians 6:14-15; 1 Corinthians 7:39)

- worried that they are not a Christian? (Philippians 1:4-6; John 11:25-26; Romans 8:38-39 and 10:9-11)

- rejected by non-Christian friends or family? (Philippians 3:20; Mark 10:29-30; John 15:18-21)

DURING
DISCIPLESHIP EXPLORED

A typical schedule

6:30 p.m.	Leader prayer
7:00 p.m.	Coffee or a meal
7:40 p.m.	Discuss any issues arising from the previous week's Follow Up
7:45 p.m.	Watch the film
8:00 p.m.	Explore Philippians
8:45 p.m.	Pray to close

Feel free to change timings or make certain sections shorter/longer depending on your situation.

So what do each of these elements look like in detail?

6:30 p.m. – Leader prayer

Pray that God will help your guest(s) grasp the truths that will be presented that week. If you have co-leaders, pray for one another too.

It can be helpful before each session to use one of Paul's prayers as a model for your own. Try praying through the following passages:

- 1 Thessalonians 5:23-24 (Session 1)
- Ephesians 1:17-19 (Session 2)
- 2 Thessalonians 1:11-12 (Session 3)
- Philemon 4-6 (Session 4)

- 2 Thessalonians 2:16-17 (Session 5)
- Ephesians 3:16-19 (Session 6)
- 1 Thessalonians 3:12-13 (Session 7)
- Colossians 1:9-12 (Session 8)

7:00 p.m. – Coffee or a meal

Eating together helps people to relax and get to know each other. The intention at this point is to share life (1 Thessalonians 2:8), not to dive straight into deep theological discussions. We want guests to know that we're genuinely interested in every aspect of their well-being. It's a great opportunity to find out about a person's hobbies, job, family, vacations, culture, and interests.

A meal is also a great opportunity to model the importance of giving thanks to God. As leader, be ready to give thanks for any food that has been prepared.

As the series progresses, ask if your guest(s) would be willing to bring some food with them next time. This is a great way to encourage participation – and also to keep some of the pressure off you.

7:40 p.m. – Discuss any issues with Follow Up

Follow Up is a short Bible-reading plan included in the Handbooks between each session. The plan is designed to help believers get into the rhythm of daily Scripture-reading, memorization, and prayer. Each session's Follow Up picks up on a relevant theme from Philippians, allowing people to discover what else Scripture has to say on that theme.

Sometimes people forget to do their Follow Up, or don't have anything they'd like to discuss, in which case, move straight on to the film.

7:45 p.m. – Film

You'll introduce the film with a simple question for your guest(s) to keep in mind as they're watching. This helps to keep people attentive, and also prepares them for the questions you'll be discussing together after the film.

(Note: You don't need to get an answer to this pre-film question – it's just for guests to keep in mind.)

Each film aims to bring a different part of Philippians into focus, showing what it teaches and what that means for us as followers of Jesus. As well as teaching from Barry Cooper, the films contain interview footage with believers from across five different continents and seven different countries, to show how Philippians has made a difference to them.

Incidentally, if you've watched the film before, it can be tempting to stop listening – but bear in mind that if leaders lose focus, guests may too.

If you register your course at **www.discipleship.explo.red/register** you'll gain access to bonus commentaries on each of the films. Each commentary features behind-the-scenes information from the creators of *Discipleship Explored* plus extra tips on running each session.

8:00 p.m. – Explore Philippians

After watching the film, you'll re-read the part of Philippians that the film was based on. Then you'll explore that part of the letter using the questions in your Handbook. The questions are designed to help people apply what's been taught in the film and delve a little deeper into Philippians.

Because some of the questions have personal applications, some people may feel shy about answering these in front of others. Giving your own answer may encourage them to do so. Otherwise, feel free to ask your guest(s) to answer the questions privately at home.

See "Some tips on leading small-group and one-to-one studies" (page 30) for more on this part of the session.

8:45 p.m. – Closing prayer

Philippians will provoke and challenge even the most mature Christian, so it's good to pray for your guest(s) at the end of the study. It's also good to model prayer for other believers. Your Leader's Handbook contains a suggested prayer, based on Paul's words in that particular part of the letter.

If it's appropriate for your guest(s), invite them to pray about what they've heard too.

The words of Martin Luther are worth bearing in mind as you pray: "One should pray short, but often and strongly; for God does not ask how much and long one has prayed, but how good it is and how it comes from the heart."

Once you've finished praying, encourage people to use the Follow Up section as their daily readings for the coming week.

Finish at the promised time. This helps to develop trust and will mean that people will be more likely to return for the next session. But let them know that they're very welcome to stay and talk further.

It's a good idea to send a message to your guest(s) during the week, to show you're praying for them, and also as a gentle reminder to complete the Follow Up. You could say something like, "I really enjoyed getting together for *Discipleship Explored*, and just wanted you to know that you're in my prayers this week. Do let me know if there's anything in the Follow Up that doesn't make sense. See you on _____."

Some tips on leading small-group and one-to-one studies

- The most important thing is your own Christ-likeness. People are as likely to be influenced by your character as by anything you might teach (Philippians 3:17).

- Be gracious and gentle, and act as peacemaker if the discussion gets heated. Remember that you're a shepherd rather than a drill sergeant.

- If a question is met with silence, don't be too quick to say something. Allow people time to think.

- If you are leading a group of people, sometimes it's good to address a question directly to an individual in order to encourage discussion (for example: "Lee, what do you think about this?").

- In a group, if one person's particular issue begins to dominate, gently ask him or her if you can talk about the issue together at the end of the session.

- Don't forget how important the tone of your voice and your body language can be as you seek to further the discussion.

- Lead honestly. You won't be able to deal with all the questions thrown your way, so don't pretend to have all the answers. Some questions can be easily addressed, but others will be difficult. If you don't know the answer, say so – but try to have an answer ready for the following week.

- During discussion you may get replies that approach the answer to a question but are not quite complete. Try to guide people from these initial answers to a better, more biblical answer. Keep pointing them back to Scripture, so that the conversation stays grounded (for example: "What does Philippians say about that?").

- Have further questions in mind to develop the initial answer (for example: "What did you mean by that?" "Where does it say that?" or, in a group setting, "What does everyone else think?").

- In group settings, if someone gives an answer that is way off track, it may be tempting to correct them immediately. Instead, try opening up the discussion by asking others what they think (for example: "Does everyone agree with Jane?").

- Don't be afraid to correct a wrong answer graciously if you think the answer will take the group too far off topic (for example: "Thank you John, that's an interesting point, but I'm not sure that's what's going on here.").

- Make sure you have people's contact details so you can send a reminder of when the next session will be. And try to keep your meeting time and place consistent – people will be much more likely to attend regularly.

In any group discussion, you're likely to meet some wonderfully different personalities:

- **The silent person** – feels self-conscious about speaking, especially in larger groups. He's best helped by encouraging people to work through each question in groups of two or three, and then having each mini-group feed their answers back to the main group.

- **The talkative person** – tends to monopolize the discussion. Depending on how well you know her, either divide the group into smaller groups to give others an opportunity to speak, or have a quiet and tactful word with her (for example: "Sue, thanks so much for everything you're contributing. I wonder if you could help me with the quieter members of the group.")

- **The arguer** – attacks the answers given by everyone else in the group. It's best to take them aside at the end of the evening and listen to any specific issues they may have. If the problem persists, it may be appropriate to remove them from the group, asking them to meet with you one to one at a different time.

- **The know-it-all** – immediately answers every question, thus stifling the group. This situation is best dealt with by supplementary questions to facilitate group discussion (for example: "Does everyone agree with Alex?").

- **The off-on-a-tangent type** – loves to steer the discussion away from the topic and talk about something entirely different. It may be that this new subject is something the whole group wants to explore, but if not, tactfully suggest that it might be good to discuss it more fully at the end of the evening.

For more on leading Bible studies, see Orlando Saer's book, *Iron Sharpens Iron: Leading Bible-Oriented Small Groups that Thrive.*

AFTER
DISCIPLESHIP EXPLORED

Discipleship Explored isn't an eight-session conveyor belt that effortlessly turns out mature Christians at the end. Even the author of Philippians knew that he wasn't yet the finished article (Philippians 3:12). Increasing Christ-likeness is an ongoing process, so once the series ends, it's good to have a deliberate follow-up strategy in place.

Stay in touch

Having spent eight sessions with your guest(s) considering profound and personal issues, you'll know them well – and they'll know you well. Under these circumstances, it would be wrong to drop them once *Discipleship Explored* finishes.

Plan to stay in touch. If it's a larger group, arrange it with your co-leaders so that each guest has at least one leader who remains in contact with him or her.

Invite your guest(s) to start coming along to church with you if they're not already regularly attending. It can be a difficult task to get people into the habit of meeting together regularly on a Sunday, but the concept of a Christian who doesn't belong to a church is foreign to the New Testament (Hebrews 10:25).

Introduce group members to other Christians and help them to become integrated within the church by joining a Bible-study group and finding an area of service within which they can participate.

Give out feedback forms

Feedback forms, given out during the last session, are a great way to challenge guests to think about what they have learned, and to help leaders plan a way forward once the series is ended.

You can download a guest feedback form from **www.discipleship.explo.red**

If you have co-leaders, it's worth asking them for feedback too. Ask them what went well, and what could be improved.

Recommend or give away books

Reading a good Christian book at the right time can be very influential. Think carefully about the books you've read to see if any of them would suit particular members of your group. If you're not an avid reader, ask around for advice about books suitable for people in different situations. You'll also find an up-to-date list of book recommendations at **www.discipleship.explo.red**

Read the Bible with a group member

Perhaps the best way to follow up *Discipleship Explored* is to suggest getting together with a person of the same sex on a regular basis to read another book of the Bible.

This can be totally informal – just two friends with an open Bible finding out what God's word has to say to them. Set the finish date in advance so neither of you feels any awkwardness about when you'll stop meeting together.

Questions to guide your study could be:

What does the passage mean?

- Are there any difficult words or ideas that merit special attention?

What does the passage mean in context?

- What comes before/after the passage?
- Why is the passage placed where it is?
- Is it addressed to a specific individual or group of people? Why?

What does the passage mean for us?

- What have we learned about ourselves?
- About God?
- How should this passage affect the way I treat God and/or people around me?

For more on reading one to one, see *One To One Bible Reading: A Simple Guide For Every Christian* by David Helm.

Pray

A supremely Christ-like way of caring for people is to pray for them. Even after *Discipleship Explored* has ended, it's important to keep praying for your guests.

For believers, pray for growth, fruitfulness, and joy. Pray especially that they will be able to put into practice what they have learned from Philippians.

If there are any who haven't yet made a commitment to Christ, pray that God would send his Spirit to open their eyes so that they would see the overwhelming beauty of Christ, and put their trust in him.

FAQS

Where should we meet?   Wherever works for the person or people you're inviting, but a quiet room in a church building or in someone's home works well.

How often should we meet?   Ideally once a week. Less often than that, and earlier sessions might be forgotten. More often than that, and it may feel a little like drinking from a fire hose.

How do I encourage people to come to Discipleship Explored?   By all means, use posters, banners, and postal invitations. You can get hold of downloadable designs from The Good Book Company.

However, by far the most effective way to get people along is one your church may already have in place: friends bringing friends.

At least six weeks in advance, show the *Discipleship Explored* trailer at your church (available online and on the *Discipleship Explored* DVD). Explain that *Discipleship Explored* has been designed to help followers of Jesus enjoy their Christian lives to the full. Share the trailer on your church website and social media if you can. Add the hashtag *#DiscipleshipExplored* so that we can mention you online.

Encourage everyone in your church family to be praying for *Discipleship Explored*, and have invitations available for church members to use.

What happens if someone isn't able to make every session?

If someone has to miss a session, they can use their Handbook to complete the session at home. Register your course to get access to the films online, which can then be shared with your guests and watched at any time.

How many leaders should there be on *Discipleship Explored*?

The best ratio is no more than three guests to one leader. If your group is mixed, it's wise to have both a male and a female leader so that one-to-one pastoral conversations can be handled appropriately.

Can I run *Discipleship Explored* one to one / in small groups / in large groups?

Yes, you can. *Discipleship Explored* is completely scalable. It can be as intimate as two people watching a film on a phone/tablet/ laptop and having a conversation in someone's home. It's also ideal for use in a small-group setting. Or you can have multiple tables of people in a larger venue, watching the films on a projector screen.

Can I give live talks in place of the films?

Yes. Film transcripts are printed in the back of this Leader's Handbook, and you're free to adapt them to your own situation.

Do I need to give people a Bible?

Each guest will need a Bible – ideally, the same translation and edition. In our experience, that makes everything run more smoothly because a) you can use page numbers when directing guests to a particular part of the Bible, and b) there won't be any confusion or off-topic discussion about the differences between Bible translations.

It's also a terrific gift for your guests, especially those who are new in the faith and don't yet have their own Bible. Low-cost Bibles are available from The Good Book Company website.

What Bible translation is *Discipleship Explored* based on?

Discipleship Explored is based on the New International Version (NIV 2011).

How can I answer tough questions?

Each person is fearfully and wonderfully made by God, each with their own story, their own suffering, and their own questions. It's vitally important, then, to be listening carefully, rather than simply waiting for a chance to recite a rehearsed answer.

That said, the "big seven" questions tend to recur frequently (especially the first one), so you should think them through before you begin *Discipleship Explored*. We give some brief pointers at the back of this Leader's Handbook (see "Questions about Christian belief," page 109).

- **What about evil and suffering?** There can't be a good and powerful God if there are evil and suffering in the world.

- **What about other religions?** There can't be only one true "way."

- **What about my freedom?** If I believe in Christianity, I become a slave because I have to follow the teaching of the Bible / the church.

- **What about hypocrisy in the church?** There are evil and intolerant people who say they're

Christians – and many good people who are not Christians – so Christianity can't be true.

- **What about judgment?** The idea that God is angry or judges people goes against the idea that God is loving.

- **What about science?** Science (especially evolutionary theory) has shown that we have no need for God or Christianity.

- **What about the Bible?** It's out of date, full of mistakes, and socially regressive.

It's a very good idea to write out briefly, in advance, how you would engage with those seven objections.

Are there any books that will help me answer tough questions?

If You Could Ask God One Question by Paul Williams and Barry Cooper is a good, entry-level treatment of the questions above.

The Reason for God by Tim Keller is more advanced but still accessible.

Can I Really Trust The Bible? by Barry Cooper is a short book that covers the most frequently asked questions about the Bible itself.

Visit **www.discipleship.explo.red** for more recommendations.

What happens if I can't answer someone's question?

It's absolutely fine to tell people that you don't know the answer to a particular question. Ask your guest(s) if it would be ok to discuss it at the next session when you've had time to give it some more thought.

What if someone asks a question that is off-topic during the session?

Thank your guest for the question, and explain that for the sake of keeping things on topic, you'd love to follow it up with them at the end of the session.

It's always tempting to try and answer every question as it comes up, but if you do, there's a good chance that a) you won't have time to complete the session in the limited time available, and b) other group members may lose interest or focus as the conversation wanders.

I'd like to know more about Philippians. Which books do you recommend?

- Sinclair Ferguson, *Let's Study Philippians*
- Gordon D. Fee, *Paul's Letter to the Philippians*
- Peter O'Brien, *The Epistle to the Philippians*

What are some good books to help Christians know Christ better?

Keep an eye on the Recommended Resources section of **www.discipleship.explo.red**. But some personal favourites would be:

- J.I. Packer, *Knowing God*
- Rankin Wilbourne, *Union With Christ*
- Stephen Smallman, *The Walk: Steps For New And Renewed Followers Of Jesus*

What are some good books to help me disciple others better?

Again, check the *Discipleship Explored* website for up-to-date recommendations, but these are excellent:

- David Helm, *One To One Bible Reading*
- Ken G. Smith, *With Him: A Biblical Model of Discipleship For Men*
- Jen Wilkin, *Women Of The Word: How To Study The Bible With Both Our Hearts And Our Minds*
- Mark Dever, *Discipling*

How can I help someone who wants to begin following Christ?

Although *Discipleship Explored* is intended for Christians, it may be that one of your guests isn't yet a follower of Jesus, and would like to be.

According to Jesus, following him begins when we "repent and believe" (Mark 1:15).

Explain that "repent" means we turn around from the direction we're currently heading in, and turn back to God. We start living life to please him, rather than continuing to rebel against him.

Explain that "believe" means we believe that Jesus is who he says he is, and that he died for our sin on the cross so that we could be reconciled to God and enjoy him forever. As a result, we're putting our trust in him and looking to obey him as our Lord and Savior.

So to repent and believe is something that we do decisively at a moment in time, but it is not just a moment to look back on. It's a new, ongoing way of life. Help your guest to see what repentance and belief will look like in their daily life:

• **A new attitude toward God.** A follower of Jesus is deeply thankful to God, and longs to know him better and love him more. This longing is nurtured by reading the Bible, praying, and spending time with his people.

Offer to read the Bible one to one with your guest.

Encourage them to pray about what they've discovered on *Discipleship Explored*, thanking God for Jesus and what he means to them. Assure them that they can speak freely in their own words, because God sees our hearts and understands our deepest longings, even if our words are hesitant and uncertain.

- **A new attitude toward God's people.** A follower of Jesus longs to love and serve their Christian brothers and sisters – and, in turn, be loved and served by them.

  This shows itself when a new believer commits themselves to a local church – a particular body of believers they can love. As Jesus said, "Love one another. As I have loved you, so you must love one another. By this everyone will know that you are my disciples, if you love one another" (John 13:34-35).

  Jesus also commanded his followers to be baptized (Matthew 28:18-20) as a way of publicly identifying with Christ and his people. Encourage your guest to speak to their pastor or minister about being baptized.

  Offer to meet your guest at church on Sunday, and help them to establish a pattern of attending each week. Encourage them to join a small group, and to use whatever skills they have in serving their brothers and sisters in Christ.

- **A new attitude toward ourselves.** A follower of Jesus longs to please him by rejecting sin and living for Jesus instead.

There will be areas of our lives which we know – or will come to see – are not pleasing to Jesus. To repent and believe means that we willingly turn away from those ways of living, and try to live life in the way God intends. This is the life Jesus described as life "to the full" (John 10:10).

• **A new attitude toward others.** A follower of Jesus seeks to love others.

We're called to reflect Christ by relating to others with love, looking for ways to treat them as we would treat ourselves: "So in everything, do to others what you would have them do to you" (Matthew 7:12). And one aspect of that love for others will be our desire to tell them the good news about what Jesus has done.

Is there a follow-up series to *Discipleship Explored*? What can we do next?

An excellent way to follow up *Discipleship Explored* is to offer to read a book of the Bible one to one with your friend. See the question above on discipling others.

If your guest isn't yet a follower of Christ, an ideal follow-up series is *Christianity Explored* or *Life Explored*. Both have been created by the team behind *Discipleship Explored*.

SECTION 2
DISCIPLESHIP EXPLORED
SESSIONS

INTRODUCTION

This section contains each of the eight sessions you'll be exploring with your guest(s). It includes all the material in their Handbook, plus additional notes and answers. Text **in bold** indicates the suggested script for leaders.

- If anyone misses a session, bring them up to speed before you start. The talk summaries will help you do this. (If you've registered your course at **www.discipleship.explo.red**, you and your guests will also have online access to the films – ideal for catching up on missed sessions.)

- Some guests may wonder how we know that the book of Philippians, or the Bible as a whole, is reliable. That's a great question to raise, but it can take a while to answer well. Either discuss it one to one at the end of the session or recommend a book such as *Can I Really Trust The Bible?* by Barry Cooper.

Key

Discuss

Watch a film

Read a Bible passage

Pray

Follow Up

SESSION 1
CONFIDENT IN CHRIST

💬 **Welcome to Discipleship Explored! We're about to see Episode 1. As you're watching, have this question in mind: "How can I be confident that I really am a follower of Jesus?" You can find that question, with space for notes, on page 7 of the Handbook.**

▷ **Confident in Christ** (Philippians 1:1-11, 14 min 36 sec)

Note: The following talk summary is on page 8 of the Handbook.

• God in his goodness is completely in control of everything – not just when things are going the way we want, but also when they aren't.

• We see this played out as Jesus was dying on the cross: the greatest imaginable good was being achieved by God even when human beings were doing their very worst.

• Because God is in control, we can be confident that nothing can prevent him from completing the good work he has begun in every believer (Philippians 1:6).

• We can be confident that God is working to change us internally if our lives start to reflect this externally.

• Because God is at work in us, we won't be passive. We'll want to respond by growing in our knowledge and love of him (Philippians 1:9-11).

Christ (v 1) | A title meaning "God's anointed one." Sometimes translated as Messiah.

God's holy people (v 1) | Those who God has set apart for himself. This is often translated as "saints." Every follower of Jesus is a saint. The collective description for God's holy people is the "church" (see Philippians 3:6 and 4:15).

Overseers and deacons (v 1) | Church leaders (1 Timothy 3:1-13).

Grace (v 2) | God's goodness to people who do not deserve it.

Gospel (v 5, 7) | The good news that Jesus Christ lived, died, was resurrected, and ascended so that we can be reconciled to God and enjoy him forever.

Day of Christ (v 6, 10) | The day when Jesus Christ will return to judge the world.

Righteousness (v 11) | Perfect goodness. To be righteous is to be "pure and blameless" (v 10). Righteousness can only come "through Jesus Christ" because only he – as God come to earth – has lived a perfectly pure and blameless life.

Let's read Philippians 1:1-11.

1. According to Philippians 1:6, what is Paul confident about?

Paul is confident that God has begun a good work in the Philippian believers, and that he will finish it. In other words, their growing Christian maturity and ultimate salvation are assured.

2. How can he be so confident? (See verse 5.)

Because of their "partnership in the gospel."

3. What do you think that phrase means, in practical terms? (See Philippians 2:25 and 4:14-16.)

The Philippians took care of Paul's needs and "shared in his troubles." This isn't just about sending money, but also care and compassion expressed in other ways.

4. So how can we be confident that God is working in us? What might that look like in your life and in your day-to-day relationships?

It's a good sign when we find ourselves wanting to serve fellow believers in our church, wanting to help share the good news about Jesus, showing hospitality, caring for others, etc.

5. **Someone might say, "If God will finish this work he started, why do I need to do anything?" What would you say to them?**

If we don't want to do anything, it's doubtful God is working in us. One of the signs God is working in us is that we have a desire to serve him (and others) better.

6. **A Christian friend is going through a tough time. They don't feel confident that God loves them and is in control of what is happening to them. Is there something from the film or our discussion that might encourage them?**

One encouragement might be Philippians 1:6: "He who began a good work in you will carry it on to completion."

Another encouragement is what happened at the cross, which is the ultimate proof of God's love for us. God the Son willingly took the punishment we deserve, so that we can be reconciled to him and enjoy him forever. He sees us as we are, yet he still loves us – enough to give up his life for us!

The cross is also the ultimate proof of God's control. Even those who killed God's Son only succeeded in bringing God's loving plan to pass. (See Acts 4:27-28.)

7. (If time) **What has been most striking for you during this session?**

This question helps you move naturally into one-to-one conversations after the session has ended.

↑ **In verse 9, Paul prays for the Philippians. Let me pray that same prayer for us now.**

Father, thank you for bringing us here today. Thank you for your great love. I pray that our love may abound more and more in knowledge and depth of insight, so that we may be able to discern what is best and may be pure and blameless for the day of Christ, filled with the fruit of righteousness that comes through Jesus Christ. We ask these things in Jesus' name and for your glory and praise. Amen.

There's a Follow Up section on page 11 of your Handbook. That's a daily plan to help us discover more about the theme of this session. Let's aim to finish that before next time and we'll discuss it then. Thank you for coming!

(Note to leader: The Follow Up studies are printed below to help you prepare for the next session.)

Paul is confident in Philippians 1:6 that God will complete the "good work" that he began in the Philippians. This "good work" is salvation. The Follow Up activities this week focus on how we can be confident of salvation.

Sunday: Think over what you heard in church this week. What did you find most helpful?

Day 1: Philippians 1:1-11 (Most Bibles have a contents page at the start to help you find particular books.)

If you can, memorize this key verse:
"He who began a good work in you will carry it on to completion until the day of Christ Jesus." (Philippians 1:6)

Day 2: Ephesians 2:8-10

1. Look at verse 8. How are Christians saved?

By grace, through faith.

2. Can Christians save themselves? Why or why not? (See verses 8 and 9.)

No. Even faith is a gift from God.

3. What cannot save us? (See verse 9.)

Our "works."

4. Are "good works" (i.e. doing good things / not doing bad things) still important for us to do? (See verse 10.)

Yes. We are "created in Christ Jesus to do good works."

If you're a Christian, thank God that he has given you the "gift" of faith (verse 8). Praise him for his amazing grace. Ask your Father for growing confidence in him, rather than in your own "works."

When you pray, one helpful model to have in mind is ACTS: **Adoration** (praising God for who he is), **Confession** (speaking honestly about what we've done wrong), **Thanksgiving** (expressing gratitude for all God is doing in your life), and **Supplication** (this is what Paul means in Philippians 4:6 when he says, "Present your requests to God").

Day 3: *"I am the way and the truth and the life. No one comes to the Father except through me."* (Jesus, speaking in John 14:6)

Think about what this verse means for you. Try to memorize it if you can.

📖 Day 4: Read Jesus' words in John 10:27-28.

In this part of John's Gospel, Jesus describes himself as "the good shepherd," and his followers are described as his "sheep."

1. In verse 27, how do "sheep" respond to Jesus?

"My sheep listen to my voice … they follow me."

2. Look at verse 28. What will Jesus give to those who follow him?

Eternal life.

3. How confident can we be of salvation, if we follow Jesus? (See verse 28.)

Very! Jesus says, "They shall never perish; no one will snatch them out of my hand."

4. Look at verse 27. What is it about us that shows we are followers of Jesus?

We listen to his voice. In other words, we obey Jesus.

Thank God for this stunning promise: "No one will snatch them out of my hand" (verse 28). If we belong to Christ, we can be sure of our salvation. We can trust him completely. He is stronger than anything or anyone else, and he will not let us go.

📖 Day 5: Re-read the passages you've read this week. Pick a verse you found particularly helpful and write it down below.

📖 Day 6: Get ready for *Discipleship Explored* by reading Philippians 1:12-26.

SESSION 2
LIVING IN CHRIST

Welcome back to *Discipleship Explored*. Before we watch the next film, does anyone have any questions from the Follow Up you did at home?

We're about to see Episode 2. As you're watching, have this question in mind: "How was Paul able to be so joyful?" You can find that question, with space for notes, on page 15 of the Handbook.

Living in Christ (Philippians 1:12-26, 11 min 28 sec)

Note: The following talk summary is on page 16 of the Handbook.

- While writing to the Philippians, Paul is under house arrest in Rome, people are trying to stir up trouble for him, and he doesn't know if he will live or die.

- And yet Paul can rejoice, because he knows that everything that's happening is actually advancing the gospel (Philippians 1:12). God is in control.

- For Paul, life is about knowing Jesus better and telling others about him.

- Because of that, even death is "gain" for Paul, because then he will "be with Christ, which is better by far" (Philippians 1:23).

- If your greatest joy in life is Jesus Christ, then nothing – not even death – can take your joy away from you.

Brothers and sisters (v 12, 14) | Christians. All Christians are part of God's family.

The Spirit of Jesus Christ (v 19) | The Holy Spirit. God sends his Spirit to help people who become Christians.

📖 **Let's read Philippians 1:12-26.**

1. Paul is torn between two extremes. What are they? (See verses 23-24.)

Life or death.

2. Why is it so hard for him to choose between the two? (See verses 22-26.)

Because if he dies, he will "be with Christ, which is better by far." But if he lives, he'll be able to continue helping the Philippians with their "progress and joy in the faith."

3. Paul's life is full of hardship, but he is full of joy (verse 18). How is that possible?

Paul is joyful because, whatever happens, the good news about Jesus Christ is being preached. Ultimately, Paul's joy comes from a relationship that cannot be shaken, not even by the worst circumstances – not even by death. "For to me, to live is Christ..." (Philippians 1:21).

4. Can you imagine how it would feel to be that joyful? If you don't feel that kind of joy, what do you think may be keeping you from rejoicing the way Paul does?

This question will help you learn more about the circumstances and challenges your guests might be facing.

SESSION 2 | **LIVING IN CHRIST**

5. **If your friends were to finish this sentence for you, what do you think they'd say about you: "For them, to live is _____ "?**

   Allow guests time to think about this for themselves, and then to share their answer with the group, if they're willing.

   If people struggle to answer, try this follow-up question: "What's the one thing that, if it was taken from you, would make you feel as if life wasn't worth living?"

6. **Given what we've learned about the source of Paul's unshakable joy, are there any changes you might make in your Christian life this week?**

   The aim of questions 5 and 6 is to help guests see that if our lives are centered on anything other than Christ, then our joy will be fragile and fleeting. For example, if someone says, "To live is playing sports," then when we lose our physical health, we'll also lose our joy in life.

   The only way we can gain the kind of joy Paul experienced is to do whatever we can to make our lives more and more about Christ. Some practical ideas might be: hearing and reading God's word more, loving and serving those in our church, sharing the gospel with others, prayer, and so on. (Your guests can find recommended reading on these subjects on the *Discipleship Explored* website: www.discipleship.explo.red)

7. **(If time) What has been most striking for you during this session?**

   This question helps you move naturally into one-to-one conversations after the session has ended.

↑ **Let's pray.**

Father, thank you for giving us Paul's life as an example. We can see that his greatest passion, his highest ambition, was to know Christ and to

59

make him known. And because of that, even when his circumstances were tough, he could still rejoice. Father, we live for lots of things and die for lots of things. Please will you change the ambitions of our hearts, by your Spirit, so that we can honestly say, "For to me, to live is Christ." In Jesus' name. Amen.

→ **There's a Follow Up section on page 19 of your Handbook. Let's aim to finish that before next time and we'll discuss it then. Thank you for coming!**

In Philippians 1:19, Paul tells the Philippians that he has been helped by their prayers and "the Spirit of Jesus Christ." This week's Follow Up activities tell us more about the Holy Spirit and what he does.

Sunday: Think over what you heard in church this week. What did you find most helpful?

Day 1: Philippians 1:12-26

If you can, memorize this key verse:
"To live is Christ and to die is gain." (Philippians 1:21)

Day 2: Ephesians 1:13-14

1. When do Christians receive the Holy Spirit? (See verse 13.)

We received the Holy Spirit when we heard and believed the gospel.

2. What does the Holy Spirit guarantee? (See verse 14.)

Our inheritance.

3. How will that truth affect your feelings, day to day, even when things are tough?

The Holy Spirit in us gives us hope. He proves we belong to God and will one day be with him.

Thank God that the Holy Spirit's presence in us guarantees that we belong to him.

Day 3: *"If you love me, keep my commands. And I will ask the Father, and he will give you another advocate to help you and be with you forever – the Spirit of truth. The world cannot accept him, because it neither sees him nor knows him. But you know him, for he lives with you and will be in you. I will not leave you as orphans; I will come to you."* (Jesus, speaking in John 14:15-18)

Thank God that if you love Jesus, you're never alone. His Spirit lives with you and in you. And he promises never to leave you.

Day 4: Galatians 5:16-23

Paul explains that inside every Christian there's a fight going on: between our sinful nature and the Holy Spirit.

1. Look at verse 16. What does it mean to "live by the Spirit?"

It means not giving in to "the desires of the flesh."

2. Looking at verses 19-21, is there anything mentioned here that you need to turn from, with the Spirit's help?

The list in verses 19-21 includes: "sexual immorality, impurity and debauchery; idolatry and witchcraft; hatred, discord, jealousy, fits of rage, selfish ambition, dissensions, factions and envy; drunkenness, orgies, and the like."

Guests may recognize that they need the Spirit's help to turn from one or more of these.

3. Looking at verses 22-23, are there ways in which you can grow, with the Spirit's help?

Verses 22-23 list the fruit of the Spirit: "love, joy, peace, forbearance, kindness, goodness, faithfulness, gentleness and self-control."

Thank God for the Holy Spirit, who gives us the power to live in the way Paul describes. Because of the Spirit, we're no longer enslaved to sin. We're free to love God and others joyfully.

Day 5: Re-read the passages you've read this week. Pick a verse you found particularly helpful and write it down below.

Day 6: Get ready for *Discipleship Explored* by reading Philippians 1:27 – 2:11.

SESSION 3
ONE IN CHRIST

Welcome back to *Discipleship Explored*. Before we watch the next film, does anyone have any questions from the Follow Up you did at home?

We're about to see Episode 3. As you're watching, have this question in mind: "What are the biggest threats to our unity with each other?" You can find that question, with space for notes, on page 23 of the Handbook.

One in Christ (Philippians 1:27 – 2:11, 14 min 48 sec)

Note: The following talk summary is on page 24 of the Handbook.

- Paul repeatedly writes about *koinonia*. This Greek word means unity, partnership, or togetherness with one another.

- When we love the brothers and sisters in our local church, it shows that we really are followers of Jesus. It also shows the world that the gospel is true and powerful (Philippians 1:27-28; John 13:35).

- But our unity is under threat by opposition from outside the church (Philippians 1:28).

- Opposition can be frightening. But like faith itself, suffering for Christ is a gift from God (Philippians 1:29). It makes us more like Jesus, and proves that we are "co-heirs" with him (Romans 8:17).

- Our unity is also under threat because of pride from inside the church (Philippians 2:3).

- Our pride is shattered if we consider the humility of Jesus. He came from the highest place, yet made himself the lowest: a slave who came to serve others by dying for them on a cross (Philippians 2:5-8).

- So in that spirit of humility, will we love and serve each other in our local church – and be of one mind with each other (Philippians 2:2)?

The gospel of Christ (v 27) | The good news about Jesus Christ.

The one Spirit (v 27) | The Holy Spirit. God gives his Spirit to all Christians.

Let's read Philippians 1:27 – 2:11.

1. **In Philippians 1:27, Paul says we should conduct ourselves "in a manner worthy of the gospel." According to Philippians 1:27 and 2:2, what does this look like?**

  - 1:27 – Stand firm in the one Spirit (that's the Spirit of Jesus, who lives in all believers). Strive together as one for the faith of the gospel.

  - 2:2 – Be like-minded, having the same love (for each other), being one in spirit and of one mind.

2. **Paul wants us to be "striving together as one for the faith of the gospel" (verse 27). What does that involve? (See Philippians 1:7, 14, 27.)**

  - Verse 7 – defending and confirming the gospel message.

  - Verse 14 – proclaiming the gospel confidently and without fear.

  - Verse 27 – living lives that are worthy of the gospel; standing firm in the Spirit of Jesus.

3. Where does this oneness come from? (See Philippians 2:1.)

Ultimately, it comes from being "united with Christ" (2:1). Logically, those who are united with Christ ought also to be united with each other. More on this later in the series.

4. Jesus commanded believers to love each other: "By this everyone will know that you are my disciples, if you love one another" (John 13:35). What might you say to a friend who said, "I love Jesus but I don't like going to church"?

People have sometimes been hurt or scarred by their experience of church, and it's good to recognize that. But as Jesus says, love for other believers – the church – is a defining mark of a true disciple. What does it say to those around us if we won't commit to loving a local church?

5. In Philippians 2:3, Paul says, "Do nothing out of selfish ambition and vain conceit. Rather, in humility value others above yourselves..." Why do you think pride is such a threat to church unity?

All kinds of answers are possible here. For example, pride makes us think we're always right. It makes us feel as if we're owed something, when actually we owe others our love and service. It makes us believe the lie that we can do without God – and without each other.

6. If even God the Son made himself "nothing" (2:7), how much more should we – as his creatures! – make ourselves nothing in the service of others? In what ways can we do that this week at our church?

Use this question to put Philippians into practice. If your group members are new to church, you may want to let them know about some of the opportunities to serve others.

7. (If time) What has been most striking for you during this session?

This question helps you move naturally into one-to-one conversations after the session has ended.

↑ **Let's pray.**

Father, thank you for the encouragement of being united with Christ, the comfort of being loved by him, and the joy of sharing in his Spirit. We're sorry that so often our pride has kept us from being truly united with our brothers and sisters in the church. Please will you give us the same mindset as Jesus, who made himself nothing, took the very nature of a servant, and humbled himself by dying on a cross. Thank you that because of this, you exalted him to the highest place. We look forward to the day when every tongue will acknowledge that Jesus Christ is Lord. In his name we pray. Amen.

→ **There's a Follow Up section on page 27 of your Handbook. Let's aim to finish that before next time and we'll discuss it then. Thank you for coming!**

In Philippians 1:27, Paul encourages followers of Jesus to "stand firm in the one Spirit, striving together as one." It's vital that we meet regularly with other believers. This week's Follow Up activities focus on that theme.

≡ **Sunday:** Think over what you heard in church this week. What did you find most helpful?

📖 **Day 1: Philippians 1:27 – 2:11**

If you can, memorize this key verse:
"Stand firm in the one Spirit, striving together as one for the faith of the gospel." (Philippians 1:27)

📖 **Day 2: Colossians 3:12-17**

1. **When "God's chosen people" meet together (verse 12), how should we treat each other? (See verses 12-14.)**

   With compassion, kindness, humility, gentleness, and patience. We should bear with each other and forgive each other. We should love one another.

2. **Look at verse 13. Why must we forgive one another?**

   Because the Lord forgave us.

3. **Where do you think we can find "the message of Christ" (verse 16)? Practically speaking, how can we "let the message of Christ dwell" in us?**

   Read and reflect on God's word, especially the good news about Jesus.

4. **Paul says that thankfulness and gratitude for what Christ has done is very important. He mentions it three times (verses 15, 16, and 17). Write down what Christ has done for you, and give thanks to him.**

   This question helps a guest remember what Christ has done for them.

Our witness to a watching world is even more powerful when they see how we love each other. Pray that God will give you a deep love for the people in your church.

Day 3: *"And let us consider how we may spur one another on toward love and good deeds, not giving up meeting together, as some are in the habit of doing, but encouraging one another – and all the more as you see the Day approaching."* (Hebrews 10:24-25)

Think of one way you can encourage a fellow believer toward love and good deeds, and do it this week. Ask God to give you strength, by his Holy Spirit, so that you can be an encouragement to a Christian brother or sister in your local church.

Day 4: 1 Peter 2:9-12

1. How does Peter describe Christians in verses 9 and 10?

A chosen people, a royal priesthood, a holy nation, God's special possession, the people of God.

2. What should Christians be doing together as a result of these descriptions? (See verse 9.)

Declaring the praises of God.

3. Why does Peter describe Christians as "foreigners and exiles" in verse 11? (See Philippians 3:20 for a clue!)

Because, as God's people, we are now citizens of heaven.

4. Look at verses 11 and 12. How should "the people of God" behave?

Abstain from sinful desires. Live good lives among those who don't believe.

5. What will be the effect when people see Christians living in this way? (See verse 12.)

Even if they accuse you of doing wrong, they will glorify God on the day he visits us.

Spend some time reflecting on your new status in Christ (verses 9-11). Thank God for these amazing truths. Ask him to give you Christian friends who can help you live a life in keeping with God's chosen people.

Day 5: Re-read the passages you've read this week. Pick a verse you found particularly helpful and write it down below.

Day 6: Get ready for *Discipleship Explored* by reading Philippians 2:12-30.

SESSION 4
OBEDIENT IN CHRIST

≡ Welcome back to *Discipleship Explored*. Before we watch the next film, does anyone have any questions from the Follow Up you did at home?

≡ We're about to see Episode 4. As you're watching, have this question in mind: "If God forgives all my sin, why does it matter how I live?" You can find that question, with space for notes, on page 33 of the Handbook.

▷ **Obedient in Christ** (Philippians 2:12-30, 17 min 18 sec)

Note: The following talk summary is on page 34 of the Handbook.

- Just as Jesus obeyed his Father, so we must obey our Father too.

- This obedience mustn't be an attempt to earn our salvation. Jesus has already earned it for us. Paul says, "Work *out* your salvation" (Philippians 2:12), not "Work *for* your salvation."

- "Religion says, 'I obey, therefore I'm accepted.' Christianity says, 'I'm accepted, *therefore* I obey.'"

- "Working out your salvation" means acting in line with your salvation. It means obeying Christ.

- Living obediently will make us "shine ... like stars" (Philippians 2:15), so that others might be attracted to Christ.

- We should be disciple-making disciples. Real disciples of Jesus want to tell others about him. As Jesus said, "The mouth speaks what the heart is full of" (Luke 6:45).

The word of life (v 16) | The word of life is Scripture; God's word; the good news about Jesus. In 1 John 1:1, Jesus is described as "the Word of life."
The day of Christ (v 16) | The day when Jesus Christ will return to judge the world.

Drink offering ... sacrifice (v 17) | In Old Testament times, an offering of wine or water was poured on top of an animal sacrifice presented to God. Paul imagines his life as a "drink offering" poured out on top of the Philippians' sacrificial service of others.

Let's read Philippians 2:12-30.

1. **Someone might say, "Jesus forgives all my sin – past, present, and future. So it doesn't really matter how I live." What would Paul say to them, based on Philippians 2:12?**

   We must work out our salvation with fear and trembling. Following Jesus isn't passive but active. We must keep on obeying him.

2. **Why do we do this "with fear and trembling"? (See verse 13.)**

   We work out our salvation in full view of God. As a result, it's right to do this with fear and trembling because God is holy: sin is an offence to him.

   As Christians, although our relationship with God is certain (Philippians 1:6), it's still possible both to please him and also to grieve him.

3. **What is it that enables us to shine "like stars in the sky," according to verses 14-16?**

   We can shine like stars by:

- verse 14 – doing everything without grumbling or arguing
- verse 15 – being blameless and pure
- verse 16 – holding "firmly to the word of life" (that is, God's word and the gospel of Jesus)

4. Why do you think Paul talks about his friends Timothy and Epaphroditus here in verses 19-30? How do they shine like stars?

They are wonderful illustrations of what it means to "shine like stars."

Notice their selflessness (verses 20-21); their desire to share the gospel with others (verse 22); their desire to take care of others (verse 25); their longing to do "the work of Christ" even if it means their lives might be at risk (verse 30).

5. Jesus commanded his followers to "go and make disciples of all nations" (Matthew 28:19). He also said, "The mouth speaks what the heart is full of" (Luke 6:45). How does the second quote help us obey the first?

Jesus says that we'll speak about what our hearts are full of. So if we fill our hearts with him, we'll speak about him more – and so help to "make disciples."

It might be worth saying that Jesus' command to "make disciples" isn't just about speaking with non-Christians. It's also about helping to build up other Christians.

6. This week, what are some practical ways we can fill our hearts with Jesus Christ so that we can help to "make disciples" of others?

This is a great opportunity to emphasize the importance of God's word, the church, and prayer as ways in which we can fill our hearts. As a leader, you could mention what you've found helpful (e.g. the sermon on Sunday, Bible-reading plans, podcasts, good Christian books, and so on.) See www.discipleship.explo.red for recommendations.

Make it clear that although the command "make disciples" can sound intimidating, it's simply helping others to follow Jesus. Ask your guest(s) to write down one person they could pray for this week – whether Christian or not – and one small step they could take to help them know Jesus better.

7. (If time) **What has been most striking for you during this session?**

This question helps you move naturally into one-to-one conversations after the session has ended.

↑ **Let's pray.**

Father, thank you that you work in us to will and to act in order to fulfill your good purpose. Thank you that it's your power that enables us to work out our salvation. Help us to do this with fear and trembling, knowing that the way we live is visible, not just to the world but also to you. We want to shine like stars so that Jesus will be more clearly seen in the places where we live and work. So please enable us to live obediently this week, by the power of your Spirit. In Jesus' name we pray. Amen.

→ **There's a Follow Up section on page 37 of your Handbook. Let's aim to finish that before next time and we'll discuss it then. Thank you for coming!**

In Philippians 2:16, Paul tells the Philippians to "hold firmly to the word of life." As we hear and obey God's word, we become more like Christ. This week's Follow Up activities focus on the theme of the Bible.

📧 **Sunday:** Think over what you heard in church this week. What did you find most helpful?

📖 **Day 1: Philippians 2:12-30**

If you can, memorize this key verse:
"Continue to work out your salvation with fear and trembling, for it is God who works in you to will and to act in order to fulfill his good purpose."
(Philippians 2:12-13)

Day 2: 2 Timothy 3:14-17

Here, Paul is writing to Timothy, the younger evangelist who helped him start the church in Philippi.

1. Look at verse 15. What are the "Holy Scriptures" able to do?

Make you wise for salvation through faith in Christ Jesus.

2. Paul wrote these words to Timothy. But where does Scripture ultimately come from? (See verse 16.)

God. It is "God-breathed."

3. What does Scripture equip a Christian to do? (See verse 16.)

Teach, rebuke, correct, and train in righteousness.

4. Look at verse 17. Why should we read the Bible?

"So that the servant of God may be thoroughly equipped for every good work."

Thank God that he reveals himself to you through his word. Ask him to help you know him better each day, and to be excited by the things he shows you as you read the word he has breathed out.

Day 3: *"Your word is a lamp for my feet, a light on my path."* (Psalm 119:105)

God's word guides us and makes us wise. It helps us know the right choices to make, and the right way to think and live. Ask God to help you trust it more and more over the coming months.

Day 4: Psalm 19:7-8

This psalm was written by David, a famous king of Israel, hundreds of years before Jesus was born.

1. What words are used to describe "the law/statutes of the Lord" (God's word) in verse 7?

Perfect and trustworthy.

2. What effect will God's word have on us if we read it? (See verse 7.)

It will refresh the soul and make wise the simple.

3. What words are used to describe God's word in verse 8?

Right and radiant.

4. How will God's word impact us if we read and obey it? (See verse 8.)

It will give joy to the heart and give light to the eyes.

Read the rest of Psalm 19, and notice all the wonderful ways in which God's word is described. Use the words of the psalm to pray your own prayer.

Day 5: Re-read the passages you've read this week. Pick a verse you found particularly helpful and write it down below.

Day 6: Get ready for *Discipleship Explored* by reading Philippians 3:1-9.

SESSION 5
RIGHTEOUS IN CHRIST

💬 **Welcome back to *Discipleship Explored*. Before we watch the next film, does anyone have any questions from the Follow Up you did at home?**

💬 **We're about to see Episode 5. As you're watching, have this question in mind: "What's wrong with our righteousness?" You can find that question, with space for notes, on page 41 of the Handbook.**

▷ **Righteous in Christ** (Philippians 3:1-9, 15 min 39 sec)

Note: The following talk summary is on page 42 of the Handbook.

- Many people, even Christians, think that God will accept them because of the good things they do, or the bad things they don't do.

- But Christianity says God accepts us because of what *Christ* has done.

- Religiously speaking, Paul had done everything right (Philippians 3:5-6).

- But now that he knows Jesus and his perfect righteousness, Paul realizes that all of his "righteousness" is actually "garbage" (Philippians 3:8).

- We desperately need a righteousness that is not our own, but comes from God. We can only get that righteousness by faith in God's Son, Jesus Christ.

- That's because he – and he alone – lived the life we should have lived. And then he – and he alone – died the death we deserve to die.

• We must "watch out" (Philippians 3:2). If we think God will accept us because of the good things we've done, we treat our Creator as if he's in our debt.

Circumcision/circumcised (v 3, 5) | For Jewish people, this is a sign that a man is one of God's people. Some taught that circumcision is necessary for a Christian to be acceptable to God, but Paul knows only Christ is necessary.

God ... Spirit ... Christ Jesus (v 3) | Scripture reveals God to be three "persons" in one: God the Father, God the Son (Jesus Christ), and God the Spirit.

Tribe of Benjamin (v 5) | All Jews came from one of twelve tribes. Benjamin was one of only two tribes that kept following God in the Old Testament.

Hebrew (v 5) | Another word for a Jewish person.

Pharisees (v 5) | A group of Jews who followed religious rules and customs very strictly.

📖 **Let's read Philippians 3:1-9.**

💬 **1. Paul lists his impressive religious qualifications in Philippians 3:5-6. What similar things do people today think will make them acceptable to God?**

Lots of possible answers here. People can start thinking they're acceptable to God because they work hard, don't break the law, and are respected in the community, or because they are morally more upright than other people. Others think they're acceptable to God because of their Bible-reading, church attendance, financial giving, baptism, taking communion or going to mass, or saying prayers, or because of a position they hold in the church, or because people admire their spiritual gifts.

2. What is Paul's view of those religious qualifications now? (See verses 7 and 8.)

Loss (verses 7-8). Garbage (verse 8).

3. Paul no longer puts any confidence in who he is or what he has done. According to verse 8, who is he placing his confidence in now – and why?

- In Christ.

- He's placing his confidence in Christ because Christ is worth so much more to him than anything else ("the surpassing worth of knowing Christ Jesus my Lord").

4. What does it mean for us as followers of Jesus to "consider everything a loss" (verse 8)? (See Luke 14:33.)

It means that we're willing to give up everything – as Paul did – because Christ is more precious to us than anything.

What this means in practice is that if we're faced with a choice between Christ and anything else, we'll choose Christ.

5. What kind of righteousness has Paul now gained, according to verse 9?

Paul has gained a righteousness that is not his own (from obeying Old Testament law), but is "the righteousness that comes from God."

6. How can you and I get this righteousness? (See verse 9.)

We get this righteousness through faith in Christ.

This is a good opportunity to clarify what faith is. Faith is:

- simply putting our trust and hope in Jesus.
- believing that he will do what he has said he will do.
- looking to him rather than ourselves.
- not a feeling.

Encourage your guests to put their faith in Christ, if they haven't done so already. See "How can I help someone who wants to begin following Christ?" on page 42 for guidance on this.

7. (If time) **What has been most striking for you during this session?**

This question helps you move naturally into one-to-one conversations after the session has ended.

Let's pray.

Almighty God, we praise you that Christ's perfect righteousness can be ours, by simple faith in him. Thank you for the example of Paul, who considered everything a loss compared to the surpassing worth of Jesus. Please help us to see that surpassing worth ourselves, to be captivated as Paul was by Christ's infinite beauty – so that we may joyfully come to reflect him more and more. We ask these things in Jesus' name and for his glory. Amen.

There's a Follow Up section on page 45 of your Handbook. Let's aim to finish that before next time and we'll discuss it then. Thank you for coming!

In Philippians 3:9, Paul speaks about "the righteousness that comes from God on the basis of faith." This week's Follow Up activities focus on the theme of righteousness.

Sunday: Think over what you heard in church this week. What did you find most helpful?

Day 1: Philippians 3:1-9

If you can, memorize this key verse:
"Not having a righteousness of my own that comes from the law, but that which is through faith in Christ." (Philippians 3:9)

Day 2: Romans 3:20-24

In this passage, "declared righteous in God's sight" (verse 20) means "made right with God." "The law" (verse 20) means God's law, the Ten Commandments.

1. Look at verse 20. What does "the law" do?

Through the law we become conscious of our sin.

2. If the law can't make us righteous in God's sight (verse 20), how can we be made righteous? (See verse 22.)

Righteousness is given through faith in Jesus to all who believe.

3. How is that made possible? (See verse 24.)

Because of what Jesus did.

God does not leave our sin unpunished: it was paid for by Jesus when he died in our place. Because of what happened at the cross, God forgives his people their sin and gives them the righteousness of Jesus. Spend some time reflecting on the wonder of this. Thank God that all who repent and believe in Jesus "are justified freely by his grace" (verse 24).

Day 3: *"God made him who had no sin to be sin for us, so that in him we might become the righteousness of God." (2 Corinthians 5:21)*

In other words, Jesus took all our sin – even our very worst sins – on himself when he died. Jesus received the condemnation we deserve, so that we would never have to. Those who are "in him" now have his righteousness. Praise and thank God for his amazing love!

📖 **Day 4: Romans 5:6-10**

1. Look at verses 6-8. What is so amazing about Christ's death?

Christ died for the ungodly; for sinners!

2. What does that prove about God's attitude toward us? (See verse 8.)

It demonstrates his love.

3. What has Jesus' death achieved for us, according to verses 9 and 10?

We are justified by his blood, saved from God's wrath, reconciled to God, and saved.

Reflect on your answer to the last question. If you're a follower of Jesus, all these things are true for you. Allow these truths to sink in and move you to worship. Pray, thanking God for all he has done for you.

📖 **Day 5:** Re-read the passages you've read this week. Pick a verse you found particularly helpful and write it down below.

📖 **Day 6:** Get ready for *Discipleship Explored* by reading Philippians 3:10-21.

SESSION 6
TRANSFORMED IN CHRIST

Welcome back to *Discipleship Explored*. Before we watch the next film, does anyone have any questions from the Follow Up you did at home?

We're about to see Episode 6. As you're watching, have this question in mind: "How can we become more like Christ?" You can find that question, with space for notes, on page 49 of the Handbook.

▷ **Transformed in Christ** (Philippians 3:10-21, 16 min 03 sec)

Note: The following talk summary is on page 50 of the Handbook.

- Jesus is more valuable to Paul than anything. Paul wants to do whatever it takes to know Jesus better and become more like him (Philippians 3:10-11).

- One of the ways we can become more like Christ is by imitating godly believers (Philippians 3:17).

- Another way in which we become more like Christ is through suffering (Philippians 3:10).

- Christ will one day return, and on that day he "will transform our lowly bodies so that they will be like his glorious body" (Philippians 3:21).

- Paul's picture of discipleship is not passive but active. We're to be like an athlete running a race, "forgetting what is behind and straining toward what is ahead" (Philippians 3:13).

- Sometimes regrets over "what is behind" can hold us back – and Paul had many reasons to regret his past.

- But believers can forget what is behind because we know that we are forgiven, and everything in our past is ultimately intended by God to make us more like Christ.

Attaining to the resurrection (v 11) | Being raised to life by Christ after death.

Let's read Philippians 3:10-21.

1. What's the one thing Paul does (according to verses 13-14), and why does he do it?

Forgetting what is behind and straining toward what is ahead, Paul "presses on" toward the goal to win the prize.

2. What are Paul's "goal" and "prize"? (See verses 10-11.)

The goal is to know Christ, and the prize is attaining to the resurrection from the dead.

3. Some might say that Christianity is just about avoiding hell and going to heaven. Given verses 10-14, what do you think Paul would say to that?

Paul certainly looks forward to heaven – "the resurrection from the dead" (verse 11) – but he would say that the greatest joy of the Christian life is knowing Christ better and becoming more and more like him.

4. In verses 18-19, Paul writes "with tears" about enemies of Christ. As well as the more obvious "enemies," this group can include those who claim to be Christian teachers but are not. How can we identify such people (see verses 18-19)?

- They're enemies "of the cross," so they deny that Jesus' death is the only way that sinners can be reconciled to God.

- Their god is their stomach, so they live to indulge their appetites (whether it be food or money or fame or sex or whatever).

- Their glory is in their shame, so they treat shameful things as if they were admirable.

- Their mind is set on earthly things, so they think only of things which have no eternal value.

5. **What are the sharp contrasts between the enemies of Christ in verse 19 and the disciples of Christ in verses 20-21?**

- Their destiny is destruction / Ours is "heaven" with bodies transformed to be like Christ.

- Their god is their stomach / Ours is "the Lord Jesus Christ."

- Their glory is in their shame / Ours is in Christ.

- Their mind is set on earthly things / We eagerly await our Savior.

6. **This week, how can we "press on toward the goal" (verse 14) of knowing Christ and becoming more like him?**

This is a good opportunity to discuss practical ways in which we can know Christ better and become more like him. If we don't make a plan, it most likely won't happen. Ideas that might come up include: forget what is behind (i.e. think about how knowing Jesus changes how we see our regrets), imitate what we see in godly believers (i.e. who would be a good role model for us in our church – who can we imitate?), meet with other people to pray or read the Bible together, speak about Jesus with friends at work or college, serve others, read a good Christian book (see recommendations on **www. discipleship.explo.red**), and so on.

7. (If time) **What has been most striking for you during this session?**

This question helps you move naturally into one-to-one conversations after the session has ended.

↑ **Let's pray.**

Heavenly Father, thank you that our citizenship is in heaven. We look forward to the day when the Lord Jesus will return and will transform our lowly bodies so that they will be like his glorious body. In the meantime, please give us a hunger to know Christ, and even to suffer for him, because that will mean we become more and more like him. Thank you that because Jesus is Lord of everything, even our past failures will be used by him to bring glory to you. So help us to forget what is behind and strain toward what is ahead, pressing on toward the goal to win the prize. In Jesus' precious name. Amen.

→ **There's a Follow Up section on page 53 of your Handbook. Let's aim to finish that before next time and we'll discuss it then. Thank you for coming!**

In Philippians 3:10, Paul speaks about his strong desire to "know Christ" and become more like him. He knows that this means he must "press on toward the goal to win the prize" (3:14). This week's Follow Up activities will help you think about what it means to "press on" and know Christ better.

≡ **Sunday:** Think over what you heard in church this week. What did you find most helpful?

📖 **Day 1: Philippians 3:10-21**

If you can, memorize this key verse:
"I want to know Christ" (Philippians 3:10).

Day 2: Matthew 6:19-24

1. Jesus tells us to store up "treasures in heaven" rather than "treasures on earth." Why? (See verses 19-20.)

Because treasures on earth will be destroyed/stolen, i.e. they don't last.

2. Look at Jesus' words in verse 21. How might we be able to tell what we really value in life?

Our "treasure" reveals what our hearts are really set on.

3. How do you use most of your time and energy? What does this show about where your heart is?

This question helps a guest apply the teaching to their own life.

4. In verse 24, Jesus says that no one can serve two masters. What are the things in your life that keep you from knowing Christ better?

This question helps a guest apply the teaching to their own life.

When Jesus says, "Store up for yourselves treasures in heaven," he is telling us to live wholeheartedly for him. There's an old poem that helps explain why this is the best way to live:

"Only one life, 'twill soon be past.
Only what's done for Christ will last."

Ask your Father to help you live for things that will last.

Day 3: *"If anyone is in Christ, the new creation has come: The old has gone, the new is here!"* (2 Corinthians 5:17)

The Christian life can be summed up in four words: "Be who you are!" Or, to put it another way, "You are now in Christ – act like it!"

Ask God for power to live a life that is more like Christ's.

Day 4: Matthew 7:24-27

1. **There are two men in this story. How does Jesus describe their characters? (See verses 24 and 26.)**

   Wise and foolish.

2. **The men both built houses, but differently. What was different about the way they built? (See verses 24 and 26.)**

   One built on rock and the other on sand.

3. **What happened to each man's house when the storm hit? (See verses 25 and 27.)**

   The house on rock stood firm. The house on sand collapsed.

4. **Why isn't it enough just to hear Jesus' words? (See verses 26-27; see also Matthew 7:21-23.)**

   We must also put Jesus' words into practice. Otherwise, any security we may feel is just an illusion.

   This doesn't mean that if we ever sin, Jesus will give up on us. Jesus intends this as a warning for those who habitually hear his words and refuse to act on them – especially those who claim to be his followers.

Many people go to church or say they are Christian, but they don't really know Christ. The mark of a genuine believer is whether or not we put God's word into practice. Only then will we be transformed more and more into the likeness of Christ.

Ask God by his Spirit to make you a person who treats Jesus not only as Savior, but also as Lord over every part of your life.

📖 **Day 5:** Re-read the passages you've read this week. Pick a verse you found particularly helpful and write it down below.

📖 **Day 6:** Get ready for *Discipleship Explored* by reading Philippians 4:1-9.

SESSION 7
REJOICING IN CHRIST

💬 Welcome back to *Discipleship Explored*. Before we watch the next film, does anyone have any questions from the Follow Up you did at home?

💬 We're about to see Episode 7. As you're watching, have this question in mind: "What should we remember if we're in conflict with another believer?" You can find that question, with space for notes, on page 57 of the Handbook.

▷ **Rejoicing in Christ** (Philippians 4:1-9, 15 min 55 sec)

Note: The following talk summary is on page 58 of the Handbook.

- Euodia and Syntyche were two Philippian believers who were in sharp disagreement with each other.

- Paul pleads with them to "be of the same mind in the Lord" (Philippians 4:2).

- That phrase, "in the Lord" or "in Christ," is key to understanding how we can be united with each other and "rejoice" (Philippians 4:4).

- The phrase "in Christ" reminds believers that we are completely united with Christ. All that is his is ours.

- Not only are we "in Christ," but he – by his Spirit – is in us.

- Remembering how rich we are in Christ means we no longer have to scrabble around after the "pennies" of approval, or power, or recognition, or getting our own way.

- We also have the privilege of praying "in Christ." The way to be anxious about nothing is to be prayerful about everything (Philippians 4:6-7).

Whose names are in the book of life (v 3) | A way of saying that these people are saved. They are genuine followers of Jesus.

Let's read Philippians 4:1-9.

1. Why do you think people tend to quarrel with one another?

There can be a lot of different reasons, but underneath them all, it's often because we're not getting something we want. For example: money, status, control, or just the recognition that we're right and the other person is wrong.

2. If those are the reasons why we quarrel with each other, how does it help to remember that we're "in the Lord" (verses 1, 2, 4)?

When we see what we already have by being "in Christ," it takes away the urge to demand what we want from others.

This question is a great opportunity to remind each other of the remarkable privileges we have because we're "in Christ." For example: his righteousness is ours (Philippians 3:9), his resurrection is ours (Colossians 3:1), and his inheritance is ours (Romans 8:17).

3. Why will remembering that "the Lord is near" (verse 5) make us gentle with others?

- "The Lord is near" reminds us that he sees all we do, so we're gentle with others because we want to please him.

- It reminds us that the Spirit of Jesus himself lives in fellow believers – and also in us.

- It reminds us that Jesus will soon return as judge. When he does, he will "repay each person according to what they have done" (Romans 2:6).

4. What action should we take when we're anxious? When should we do it, and why? (See verses 6-7.)

We should pray "in every situation," with thanksgiving, so that our anxiety will be replaced by "the peace of God," which will guard our hearts and minds "in Christ Jesus."

5. How will praying in that way make us feel like rejoicing "in the Lord"?

When we pray "with thanksgiving," we're remembering all the blessings that we have "in Christ" – and that causes us to be joyful!

We're also reminded of the one we're praying to: we remember that he loves us as a father dearly loves his child, and that he withholds no good thing from us (Psalm 84:11).

6. Read verses 8-9. How can we put these verses into practice this week?

Encourage group members to give practical answers here. For example, what will we do (or not do) so that our minds are filled with these good things? Since everything in verse 8 is true of Jesus himself, how can we spend time glorying in him this week?

7. (If time) What has been most striking for you during this session?

This question helps you move naturally into one-to-one conversations after the session has ended.

↑ **Let's pray.**

Heavenly Father, thank you for teaching us how to pray: that we should always pray with thanksgiving, remembering all you have done for us "in Christ." Thank you that because of your tender and unchanging love for us, we can rejoice in you always. Keep us from quarreling with each other, as we remember how rich we are in Christ. We pray in his precious name. Amen.

↪ **There's a Follow Up section on page 61 of your Handbook. Let's aim to finish that before next time and we'll discuss it then. Thank you for coming!**

In Philippians 4:6, Paul says, "Do not be anxious about anything, but in every situation, by prayer and petition, with thanksgiving, present your requests to God." There's a close connection between how much we pray and how much we rejoice. So this week's Follow Up activities focus on prayer.

≡ **Sunday:** Think over what you heard in church this week. What did you find most helpful?

📖 **Day 1: Philippians 4:1-9**

If you can, memorize this key verse:
"Rejoice in the Lord always. I will say it again: Rejoice!" (Philippians 4:4)

📖 **Day 2: Colossians 1:3-14**

In this passage, Paul prays for the Christians living in a place called Colossae.

1. **What emotion does Paul express as he prays for these Christians? (See verse 3. Clue: He feels the same way when he prays in Philippians 1:3-4.)**

   Gratitude, joy, thanks.

2. **Look at verse 9. How often does Paul pray for the Colossians?**

   Very often! He says, "We have not stopped praying for you."

3. **What does Paul pray for the Colossians? (See verses 9-10.)**

   That God would fill them with the knowledge of his will through all the wisdom and understanding that the Spirit gives, so that they would live a life worthy of the Lord.

4. **What can you learn from Paul about how to pray for yourself and others?**

   This question helps a guest apply the teaching to their own life.

   None of Paul's prayers for his friends contain an appeal for God to change their circumstances. Could there be a lesson for us here? As you pray now, put into practice what you've just learned from the way Paul prays.

Day 3: *"If you, then, though you are evil, know how to give good gifts to your children, how much more will your Father in heaven give good gifts to those who ask him!"* (Jesus, speaking in Matthew 7:11)

Jesus says that even a sinful, earthly father knows how to give good gifts to his children. Imagine, then, how much more your perfect Father in heaven will give his children good gifts if they ask him!

Ask your Father for whatever "good gifts" you need. Remember that what we want is not always what we need. If you have not been given something you want – even desperately want to the extent of feeling that you need it – your loving Father has something better in mind for you.

"Everything is needful that he sends; nothing can be needful that he withholds." (John Newton)

Day 4: Matthew 6:5-13

In this passage, Jesus himself teaches his disciples how they should pray.

1. What kinds of things should we avoid when we pray? (See verses 5-8.)

- Hypocrisy – praying as a way of seeming godly to others.
- Babbling - thinking God will hear us because of our long, flowery prayers.

2. Look at verses 9-10. What is the first thing Jesus tells the disciples to do as they pray? (Note: "Hallowed" means "highly honored.")

We should honor our Father, asking that his will be done.

3. How different is this from the way that you usually pray?

This question helps a guest apply the teaching to their own life.

4. In verses 11-13, Jesus teaches us to pray for three things in particular. What are they?

That God will provide for us (v 11). That he will forgive us (v 12). That he will keep us from temptation (v 13).

5. If "your Father knows what you need before you ask him" (Matthew 6:8), why do you think Jesus tells us to pray?

Because even though God is completely in control of the world, he wants us to feel the pleasure of sharing with him in his work. Prayer also deepens our trust and joy in our heavenly Father.

Pray now, rejoicing that your Father in heaven hears you and loves to hear your prayers.

Day 5: Re-read the passages you've read this week. Pick a verse you found particularly helpful and write it down below.

Day 6: Get ready for *Discipleship Explored* by reading Philippians 4:10-23.

SESSION 8
CONTENT IN CHRIST

🔲 Welcome back to *Discipleship Explored*. Before we watch the next film, does anyone have any questions from the Follow Up you did at home?

🔲 We're about to see the last episode. As you're watching, have this question in mind: "What's the secret of contentment?" You can find that question, with space for notes, on page 67 of the Handbook.

▷ **Content in Christ** (Philippians 4:10-23, 17 min 54 sec)

Note: The following talk summary is on page 68 of the Handbook.

- What is the one thing you feel you lack that would finally bring you contentment?

- Paul knew that deep contentment can be experienced regardless of how much we have or how little (Philippians 4:11-12) – because it's found in Christ (Philippians 4:13).

- The Philippians understood how "rich" they were in Christ, and this awareness enabled them to support Paul generously and self-sacrificially (Philippians 4:14-16).

- They also knew from their own experience that "it is more blessed to give than to receive" (Acts 20:35).

- We'll finally discover the secret of contentment when we become "like a weaned child" (Psalm 131:2) – always trusting our Father completely even though, like a child, we won't always understand everything he does.

- Lasting contentment only comes when we've learned to trust that our Father holds us in his arms, intends everything – even our suffering – for our good, and will meet our deepest needs "in Christ Jesus" (Philippians 4:19).

Macedonia (v 15) | Philippi was in Macedonia, part of ancient Greece. See map on page 79 of guest Handbook or 17 of this Handbook. **Thessalonica (v 16)** | Another city in Macedonia.

Amen (v 20, 23) | A Hebrew word meaning "truth" and "certainty." The word "amen" confirms that what has just been spoken is true.

Let's read Philippians 4:10-23.

1. If you're being honest, how would you finish this sentence: "I can be content, as long as _____ "?

This is another way of asking the question in Session 2: "If your friends were to finish this sentence for you, what do you think they'd say about you: 'For them, to live is _____'?"

The question may reveal where guests are struggling to trust Christ fully. Answers can be a useful starting point for a one-to-one conversation after the session has ended.

2. If we currently feel discontent, what would Paul say to encourage us? (See Philippians 4:11-12.)

Being content isn't dependent on gaining something we don't currently have. He has learned to be content whatever his circumstances – both in need and in plenty – and we can too.

3. Where does Paul find true contentment, according to Philippians 4:13? (See also 1:21, 3:10-11 and 4:7.)

In Jesus Christ.

4. Paul is in chains as he writes. He's been "hungry" and "in want," and has had many "troubles" (4:12, 14). Yet he is content in Christ. Briefly skim through Philippians to find some of the things that make this possible.

Here are some of the answers that people might give. Don't feel you have to mention everything in this list.

- Paul's confident that Christ will finish the work he's begun in him (1:6).
- He knows that the Lord Jesus is in control of all his circumstances, so that even bad circumstances are working together for good (1:12).
- His greatest joy in life is Christ (3:8), and not even death can rob him of that (1:21).
- He knows that his salvation rests securely on what Christ has done – not on anything he himself has done (3:8-9).
- His purpose in life is to become more like Christ, and suffering only helps him achieve that aim (3:10-11).
- He knows his citizenship is in heaven (3:20), and that his name is in the book of life (4:3).
- He knows that Christ will return and transform Paul's lowly body so that it will be like Christ's glorious body (3:21).
- He knows the comfort of Jesus' Spirit (4:5).
- He remembers that the Lord Jesus will return (4:5).
- He has the privilege of being able to speak directly to God himself (4:6).
- He knows that the peace of God will be with him as he obeys (4:7, 9).
- He knows that God will meet all his needs according to the riches of his glory in Christ Jesus (4:19).

5. Which of these realities do you most struggle to believe?

This is a chance to discover where your guests feel they're most likely to need spiritual help once *Discipleship Explored* is finished.

6. Now that *Discipleship Explored* is finished, what steps would you like to take next? Are there any resolutions you'd like to make, or is there anything your brothers and sisters in Christ could help you with?

Here's a chance to translate into action what we've seen in Philippians. Perhaps some would like to read the Bible with you one to one, or meet up regularly with others to pray, or find some way in which they can meet the needs of others at church.

After praying at the end of the session, make sure you, or a co-leader if more appropriate, have contact details for your guest(s). Get a future date in the calendar when you can meet them individually to find out how they're doing.

7. (If time) **What has been most striking for you during this session?**

This question helps you move naturally into one-to-one conversations after the session has ended.

We've seen that Jesus calls his disciples to make disciples of others. So now we're at the end, I'd love to give away my Leader's Handbook and the films to anyone who'd like them. The one condition is that you use them to go through DE with another Christian. Would anyone like to do that?

Let's pray.

Almighty God, Heavenly Father, Creator of all comfort and contentment, thank you that you've brought us together over these past weeks. Thank you that you know us intimately and love us completely. You know all of our troubles and all of our joys. Thank you that in Christ we can experience contentment in every situation, in every circumstance. Please help us to encourage one another in these coming weeks. And by your Spirit, make us more and more content as we grasp "the riches of God's glory in Christ Jesus." In Christ's name we pray. Amen.

There's a final Follow Up section on page 71 of your Handbook. Thank you for coming!

Paul ends his letter to the Philippians by speaking about contentment. He says, "I have learned to be content whatever the circumstances" (Philippians 4:11) – and this comes from a man who is in chains! As we reach the end of *Discipleship Explored*, the Follow Up activities this week focus on how we can remain content, even in difficult circumstances.

Sunday: Think over what you heard in church this week. What did you find most helpful?

Day 1: Philippians 4:10-23

If you can, memorize this key verse:
"I have learned the secret of being content in any and every situation."
(Philippians 4:12)

Day 2: 1 Timothy 6:6-12

Paul is writing to Timothy, the younger evangelist who helped him start the church in Philippi.

1. **Paul says, "Godliness with contentment is great gain. For we brought nothing into the world, and we can take nothing out of it" (verses 6-7). Are you living for something that you can't take with you? How might that affect your contentment?**

The question helps your guest apply the teaching to their own life.

2. Look at verses 9-10. What else might keep us from being content?

Love of money.

3. What should we do instead, if we want to be content? (See verses 11-12.)

Pursue righteousness, godliness, faith, love, endurance, and gentleness. Fight the good fight of faith. Take hold of the eternal life to which you were called.

It's very hard to just stop loving money and earthly things. Desire for those things needs to be driven out by love for something – or someone – greater.

Ask God to give you a love for Jesus that is more powerful than your love for earthly things. Ask him to open your eyes so that you can see how much more desirable Christ is than anything else.

Day 3: *"Follow God's example, therefore, as dearly loved children and walk in the way of love, just as Christ loved us and gave himself up for us as a fragrant offering and sacrifice to God."* (Ephesians 5:1-2)

Following Christ means following his lead in every area of your life. Ask your Father in heaven for strength to "walk in the way of love," just as your Lord and Savior did.

Day 4: Colossians 3:1-10

Paul says that it's not enough for us to have "taken off" our old selves (verse 9). We must also "put on the new self" (verse 10) if we are to experience the contentment Christ brings.

1. **Paul says, "Set your hearts on things above, where Christ is." In other words, Christians should desire and live for those things that are Christ-like. Why is that? (Look at the beginning of verse 1.)**

   Because we've been raised with Christ.

2. **What does that mean? (See verse 4.)**

   When Christ returns, we will "appear with him in glory."

3. **How should Christians live in the light of that fact? (See the start of verse 5.)**

   Put to death whatever belongs to the earthly nature.

4. **Look at verses 5-10. Make a list of the things Paul tells us to turn away from.**

   "Sexual immorality, impurity, lust, evil desires, and greed … anger, rage, malice, slander, and filthy language … lie[s]."

5. **What will your "new self" (verse 10) look like? Write down words that are the opposite of the ones you wrote down in question 4.**

   Sexual morality, purity, love, godly desires, generosity, good humor, peacemaking, kindness, honesty, loving language, and truthfulness.

Your contentment as a Christian will depend on setting your heart on things above (verse 1). Pray that God's Holy Spirit will give you power and self-control to take off the old self and put on the new. Ask your loving Father to give you deep, lasting contentment as you do that.

Day 5: Spend some time looking back over these Follow Up activities. What can you thank God for? In what ways can you ask his Spirit to help you grow? Pray about these things, thanking him for all he's done for you in Jesus.

Day 6: Philippians 1:9-11 gives you an idea of what Paul, if he were here, might pray for you right at this moment:

"This is my prayer: that your love may abound more and more in knowledge and depth of insight, so that you may be able to discern what is best and may be pure and blameless for the day of Christ, filled with the fruit of righteousness that comes through Jesus Christ – to the glory and praise of God."

So, what happens next?

• Keep reading!

Keep going with your Bible-reading, so that "your love may abound more and more in knowledge and depth of insight." The book of James is a great follow-up to Philippians. Why not start to read that, beginning tomorrow?

• Keep praying!

The most joyful Christians are prayerful Christians, because through prayer we become even closer in our friendship with Christ. Paul usually begins his letters with a prayer, and the prayers begin with thanks and gratitude for what God has done. That's a great thing for us to copy as we pray.

• Keep meeting!

Keep meeting regularly with other Christians. The Holy Spirit gives every Christian "spiritual gifts." He gives these gifts so that we can strengthen other believers, and so that others can do the same for us (1 Corinthians 12:7). So "stand firm in the one Spirit, striving together as one for the faith of the gospel" (Philippians 1:27). And be encouraged. We're praying for you.

"Finally, brothers and sisters, whatever is true, whatever is noble, whatever is right, whatever is pure, whatever is lovely, whatever is admirable – if anything is excellent or praiseworthy – think about such things. Whatever you have learned or received or heard from me, or seen in me – put it into practice. And the God of peace will be with you." (Philippians 4:8-9)

APPENDICES

QUESTIONS ABOUT
CHRISTIAN BELIEF

How do you know that God exists?

- Many philosophical and scientific arguments have been used over the years to show that believing in God is rational and sensible. But ultimately, even the best of these lead only to general belief in a God, and not necessarily in the God spoken of in Scripture. It is usually more helpful to talk about Jesus and his claim to be God.

- We can know God exists because he became a man: Jesus Christ. This is the core of Jesus' answer to Philip's question in John 14:8-9. It's worth looking this up and reading it together if the question arises.

- Jesus was a real person who lived in Palestine 2,000 years ago – the historical evidence for this stacks up (see next question).

- Jesus claimed to be God (e.g. John 5:18; 20:28-29). If those claims are borne out by Jesus' life, then that would be the strongest possible proof that God does indeed exist.

Why should we believe what the Bible says?

- Again, our answer to this question will depend on our view of Jesus. What's clear from the Gospels is that Jesus trusted the Scripture implicitly. So, if we believe Jesus himself is trustworthy, it follows that Scripture is trustworthy.

- Try not to get bogged down in defending passages from all over the Bible. Instead, for the sake of clarity, focus on the reliability of the Gospels. If what they contain about Jesus is reliable, then his words about the trustworthiness of Scripture as a whole come into play.

- The Gospels were written within living memory of the public events they record. Yet none of the first readers were able to disprove the claims made about Jesus' life, death, and resurrection.

- Textual criticism shows that the text of these documents has come down to us intact from the era in which they were written.

- The New Testament writers kept insisting on the truth of the history they'd recorded, even though they knew it would likely lead to persecution, torture, and death. They were so convinced they had seen and touched and interacted with Jesus, after he had been publicly executed and buried, that they were prepared to die rather than lie about what they'd witnessed.

- The Gospels are very uncomplimentary about the disciples who assisted in writing them. For example, Peter helped Mark write his Gospel – and yet Peter is shown to be a coward (Mark 14:66-72). Given that Peter was a leader in the early church, why would Mark include something like this? Unless, of course, it was just the inconvenient truth.

- The Gospel accounts are too detailed to be legends. They're packed full of tiny details that apparently serve no purpose, unless explained simply as eyewitness details. Modern novels sometimes have this level of detail, but they didn't exist until about 300 years ago; it's unprecedented in an ancient document. The author C.S. Lewis (formerly Professor of English Literature at both Oxford and Cambridge) said, "I have been reading poems, romances, vision literature, legends, and myths all my life. I know what they are like. I know none of them are like this."

- For more detail on these and other Bible-related questions, Barry Cooper's *Can I Really Trust The Bible?* is a brief, accessible read aimed at both Christians and non-Christians.

Isn't the Bible out of date socially, culturally, and sexually?

- If the Bible is a product of its time and place, aren't we also products of our time and place? For example, social and sexual ethics that seem self-evidently true to a 21st-century person living in London aren't self-evidently true to most people currently living in Nairobi – or those who were living in London 50 years ago. How can we be sure that we, in our own particular time and place, know best?

- If we feel discomfort at some of the Bible's teaching, is it really because the Bible is a product of its time, or because we are?

- If the Bible really were God's word, wouldn't it be highly suspicious if it always happened to agree with us on our particular views, in our particular moment of history?

Don't all good people go to heaven?

- What is "good"? How good is "good enough"?

- Some of us are better than others, but no one meets God's standards (see Romans 3:23).

- We are not good, because our hearts are "sin factories" (Mark 7:21-22).

- People who think they're good enough for heaven don't realize that they've broken what Jesus calls the first and most important of all God's commands: "Love the Lord your God with all your heart and with all your soul and with all your mind and with all your strength" (Mark 12:28-30). Rather than loving God, we love other things more (see the story of the rich man meeting Jesus in Mark 10:17-22). We may be "good" relative to others, but we can't be good enough for heaven if we break God's most important command.

- The opposite is, in fact, true. "Good" people go to hell; bad people go to heaven. Those who think they are good, and rely on that, will be lost. Only those who know they are lost are able to receive forgiveness and eternal life from Christ.

Why would a good God send people to hell?

- God is utterly holy and good. His character is what decides right and wrong in the universe.

- God must judge everyone. He would not be a just God if he ignored wrongdoing or evil. He will judge fairly and well.

- We know that punishments ought to fit the crime. Someone who murders deserves a worse punishment than someone who runs a red light. Is it possible that the reason we think hell is unfair is because we don't realize how serious our sin is?

- Jesus is the most loving person who has ever lived, but it is he who teaches most about the reality of hell. He does so because he knows it is real, and he doesn't want us to suffer the inevitable consequences of our rebellion against God.

- When Jesus died on the cross, he was dying in our place. For those who turn to him, Jesus took the punishment we deserve, so we can know God and enjoy him forever. Jesus went through hell, so we don't have to.

- If we understood how holy God is, we would be asking the opposite question: how can God allow anyone into heaven?

If God forgives everything, does that mean I can do what I like?

- God offers us forgiveness so that we can know and enjoy him. Why would we want to do what we like if doing so keeps us from enjoying him to the full, and puts us in danger of judgment?

How can we be sure that there is life after death?

- Scripture teaches that everyone will be resurrected after death in order to face judgment (Hebrews 9:27). For those who know and love Christ, there is nothing to fear, because the One appointed as Judge (Acts 17:31) is also the One who gave his life for them.

- Who do you trust for accurate information about life beyond the grave? The person who has been there and come back. If Jesus has been raised from the dead, then those who trust in him will also be delivered from death. (See John 11:25.)

What about other religions?

- Sincerity is not truth. People can be sincerely wrong.

- If the different religions contradict each other (which they do at several major points), they cannot all be right.

- The question really is: has God revealed himself, and if so, how? Jesus claimed to be the unique revelation of God. He claimed to be God in the flesh. Are his claims valid? If Jesus is God, then logically, other religions must be wrong.

- Jesus claims he is the only way (John 14:6).

- Religions can do many good things: provide comfort, help, social bonding, etc. But all of them – apart from Christianity – teach that we must DO something in order to "earn" our place in heaven.

- By contrast, Jesus claims that we can never earn our way to heaven by doing good things. He claims that the only way we can know and enjoy God forever is if we trust in what HE (Jesus) has done on our behalf, not in what WE have done.

What about those who have never heard about Jesus?

• We can trust God to be just; he will judge people according to their response to what they know.

• Everyone has received some revelation about God, even if only from the created world (see Romans 1:18-19).

• Those who have had more revealed to them will be held more responsible (Matthew 11:20-24).

• We have heard, so we must do something about it – and leave others to God, who will treat them fairly.

Isn't faith just a psychological crutch?

• It is true that faith in Christ provides an enormous psychological crutch! It gives hope, meaning, and joy, even in the face of suffering and death. It is life's greatest joy to know for certain that you are perfectly known and yet perfectly loved by the Creator of the universe.

• But that doesn't mean Christian faith is wishful thinking – a belief in imaginary stories created to make us feel better in the face of life's hardships.

• On the contrary, Christian faith is founded on historical events: the life, death, and resurrection of Jesus. The truth of these events – and therefore the truth of Christianity – doesn't depend on whether or not we need them to be true.

Why would I give up my freedom to follow Christ, or anyone else?

• Don't we know from our own experience that to enjoy certain freedoms, we must give up others? The skier who wants to enjoy the freedom of the slopes must give up the "freedom" to ignore the warning signs at the cliff edge. The person who wants to enjoy the freedom and security that comes from a good marriage must give up certain freedoms they may have had as a single person.

• In the same way, Jesus said that true freedom only comes from following him. This is because "everyone who sins is a slave to sin" (John 8:34), and Christ is the only one who can release people from that slavery: "If you hold to my teaching … you will know the truth, and the truth will set you free" (John 8:31-32).

Why does God allow suffering?

• Much suffering is a direct result of our own sinfulness (e.g. that caused by drunkenness, greed, lust, etc.).

• But some is not (see John 9:1-3).

• All suffering results from the fallen nature of our world (see Romans 8:18-25).

• God uses suffering to discipline and strengthen his children (see Hebrews 12:7-11; Romans 5:3-5).

• God also uses suffering to wake people up so that they understand that there is a judgment coming to our pain-filled world (Luke 13:1-5).

• Unlike many other "gods," the God of the Bible knows intimately what it is like to suffer. God the Son suffered loneliness, grief, temptation, alienation from loved ones, mockery, isolation, bereavement, hunger, thirst, homelessness, mental anguish, and the worst physical agonies humans have been able to invent. As a result, he relates to and sympathizes with our deepest pain (Hebrews 4:15). He is not distant from it or disinterested in it.

- But the God of the Bible does more than show mere sympathy; he has done something decisive to end all human suffering. Jesus suffered and died so that those who know and love him can one day enjoy a new creation, where there will be no suffering or pain of any kind.

- Though we don't know all the reasons why God allows suffering in every case, it seems reasonable to assume that our not knowing doesn't necessarily mean suffering must be pointless. At the time Jesus suffered and died, the disciples would have felt that his death was a horrible evil, a pointless tragedy. And yet, if the biblical claim is true, his suffering and death were the means by which countless millions of lives have been saved.

- "With time and perspective most of us can see good reasons for at least some of the tragedy and pain that occurs in life. Why couldn't it be possible that, from God's vantage point, there are good reasons for all of them?" (Tim Keller)

Hasn't science disproved Christianity?

- It's good to clarify what is meant by the question. There may be some specific issue which needs addressing – and that will require some research. But during the session, it's best to avoid having technical discussions about evolution, carbon dating, etc. as you're likely to run over time and leave other members of the group feeling bored or excluded.

- Most people mean, "Hasn't the theory of (macro) evolution replaced the idea of creation, and so disproved Christianity?" (Usually, people aren't talking about science such as archaeology which, incidentally, backs up Scripture at almost every point.)

- Ask what conclusions are being drawn from evolution. Does it give an account of how life came to be in the first place? How did something come from nothing – literally nothing, not even empty space? Does evolutionary theory answer the questions of WHY things exist, what is the purpose of life, what should we live FOR?

- If Jesus is God, it puts the creation/ evolution debate into a completely different perspective. So it's usually more fruitful to begin by addressing those issues first (see above question on the existence of God).

If Jesus is God's Son, how can he be God too?

- Jesus lets himself be described as the "Son of God" – a term which can mean that he is the King of God's people, but can also be a claim that he is much more.

- Jesus acts in the New Testament in the way that God does in the Old Testament. He speaks as God speaks, and does things that only God can do (raises the dead, forgives sins, controls nature, etc.). His words and actions show that he is making a claim to be God.

- Christians do not believe that there are many gods, and that Jesus is just one of them. Scripture teaches that God is a "tri-unity" or "Trinity": one God in three "persons." The three persons are Father, Son, and Spirit, all of whom are fully God. For one example of this biblical teaching, see the description of Jesus' baptism in Mark 1:10-11, where God's tri-unity is clearly seen.

- This is complex and hard to grasp fully – but wouldn't it be strange if the nature of God himself were an easy thing for finite humans to understand?

Why does God hate sex?

- It would be odd if the Creator of sex hated it! He created sex to be beautiful, enjoyable, and extremely powerful.

- Isn't it likely that our Creator knows best what leads to our joy and health? He designed sex to be enjoyed by a husband and wife within the mutual protection of marriage (see Jesus' words in Matthew 19:4-6). Sex joins people together in a way that is more than physical.

- Marriage is a temporary institution which anticipates and reflects a far greater marriage: the marriage of God and his people, which God's people will enjoy in the new creation. This is why Jesus is described as the bridegroom and

his people are portrayed as his bride (Revelation 19:7-9).

- But those who, for whatever reason, remain single all their lives will not miss out on anything if their hope is in Christ. Not even the very best earthly marriage will come close to the experience of being fully known and loved in the new creation (Revelation 19:7-9).

Christians are hypocrites – so how can Christianity be true?

- The failure of many Christians to live according to their stated beliefs does not invalidate Jesus' claims to be God.

- Scripture says that Jesus alone is perfect, and it is honest about the failures and weakness of his followers.

- Jesus taught that there will always be false teachers and fakes (Mark 13:21-22) who pretend they are Christians but who are not. This is true today.

- Everyone is a hypocrite to some extent. How many of us fully and perfectly "practice what we preach?" But Jesus calls those who follow him to grow more like him.

Note: For more answers to these and other questions, see *If You Could Ask God One Question* by Paul Williams and Barry Cooper. It's ideal for leaders and for group members. More technical but still very readable is *The Reason for God* by Tim Keller.

QUESTIONS ABOUT
PHILIPPIANS

Philippians 1:1
Why does Paul call Jesus "Christ Jesus," not "Jesus Christ"?
Jesus (meaning "God saves") is the human name given to the Son of God when he was born to Mary. Christ is his title, meaning "anointed one" or "chosen one." In Greek, as in English, a change in word order can reflect a slight change in emphasis.

Notice the way in Philippians 2:5-11 that Paul starts with "Christ Jesus" and ends with "Jesus Christ." This fits perfectly with Paul's theme in this section – it begins with Christ humbling himself as a man, and ends with the man Jesus being exalted in glory.

Philippians 1:5
What does Paul mean by their "partnership in the gospel"?
The gospel had made Paul and the Philippians "partners" with each other, and the lives of the Philippians reflected that reality. For example:

- **Acts 16** – Lydia, one of the first believers in Philippi, opened her home to Paul, as did the jailer who previously had been charged with guarding Paul while he was in prison there.

- **Philippians 2:25** – They had sent one of their members – Epaphroditus – to look after Paul's needs.

- **Philippians 4:15-18** – They were the only church that had sent Paul money and gifts to support him when he set out from Macedonia.

This visible love for Paul, and for one another, demonstrated that they were genuine followers of Christ. If someone had said to Paul that they loved Jesus but preferred to stay away from their local church, he would have had little confidence that such a person knew Christ at all.

Philippians 1:6
What is "the day of Christ Jesus"?
"The day of Christ Jesus" (v 6) and "the day of Christ" (v 10) both mean the day when Christ will return to judge the world. The Bible makes it clear that this day will certainly come, but that we do not know when it will be (Matthew 24:36-44).

Philippians 1:11
What does "righteousness" mean?
One simple way to explain this is to say that righteousness is having a "right standing" with God. However, it's important to distinguish between two different uses of the word:

1. Christ gifts his righteousness to those who believe in him. Jesus is the only

person who ever lived a truly righteous life, and when someone becomes a follower of Christ, Jesus credits them with his righteousness. That means that when God looks at a Christian, he sees the goodness and purity of his Son. We're forgiven by him, freed from his condemnation, adopted by him, and loved by him.

2. Christians should try to live righteous lives. As we grow in our faith, we want to be more like Jesus. We aim to be more holy, pure, and righteous. However, this righteousness can't save us. It isn't the *reason* for our salvation; it's the *response* to it.

Philippians 1:18
Why is Paul content with people preaching Christ from false motives when he so clearly condemns false teachers in chapter 3?
Paul's whole life is focused on knowing Christ and making him known. The fact that he is overjoyed at the preaching of Christ by these rivals shows that the gospel they are preaching must be the true one, even if they are doing so out of a personal hostility toward Paul. So the apostle doesn't really care if he is in prison, or that others have it in for him. He is overjoyed that the gospel is being heard.

Philippians 1:19
What is "God's provision of the Spirit of Jesus Christ"?
God's Spirit helps us in many ways. For example:

• The Holy Spirit changes us to become more like Jesus (Galatians 5:22-23).

• He helps us to pray (Romans 8:26-27).

• The Holy Spirit helps us to be bold in telling others the good news about Jesus Christ (Acts 4:31).

• He fills us with wisdom and understanding, so that we come to know God better and find out how he wants us to live (Colossians 1:9-10).

Philippians 1:19
What does Paul mean by "deliverance"?
This cannot mean deliverance from prison, because that would make the sentence contradictory: how could "what has happened to me" (i.e. prison) "turn out for my deliverance" (i.e. release from prison)? The word translated "deliverance" is *soteria*, which is usually translated "salvation."

Philippians 1:27
What does "worthy of the gospel" mean?
We can't make ourselves "worthy" to receive the gospel and salvation. Paul means that, having been adopted by God, we should live in a way that is consistent with being his children.

Philippians 1:27
What does "stand firm in the one Spirit" mean?
When a lump of coal falls out of a fire, it quickly goes cold. It only continues to burn and give off heat when it's in the fire with other pieces of coal. In the same way, when we're part of a local fellowship of believers, loving and supporting one another, we'll be healthy and effective disciples. But if we stay away and try to go it alone, our "heat" as Christians rapidly wanes.

As Hebrews 10:24-25 says, "Let us consider how we may spur one another on toward love and good deeds, not giving up meeting together, as some are in the habit of doing, but encouraging one another."

Philippians 1:28

What is the "sign to them that they will be destroyed, but that you will be saved"?

When disciples stick together and support one another in their work for the gospel, it is a sign that they genuinely belong to Christ. It is part of the "fruit of righteousness" (1:11). It is one of the outward signs of the inner change that God is working in you. It is a sign that you will be saved by God on the day of Christ (1:6, 10) – when everyone in the world will be judged.

If someone is opposed to believers, this shows that they are not in Christ. Therefore they will not be saved, but destroyed. This is how Paul himself once was – persecuting Christians! But God saved even him – the "worst" of sinners (1 Timothy 1:15-16).

Philippians 2:1

What does Paul mean by "common sharing in the Spirit"?

All believers receive – and share in – the same Holy Spirit, and so (Paul argues) they should be like-minded and love each other.

Philippians 2:10

Why will "every knee" bow to Jesus?

This cannot mean that everyone will one day come to faith. Isaiah 45:22-24 makes clear that although all will bow, those who are rebellious will still "be put to shame" at judgment.

Philippians 2:12

What does it mean to "work out your salvation"?

Notice that Paul does not say "work for your salvation." Salvation has already been bought by the death of Jesus. Paul's phrase refers to the way in which we live in the light of that salvation.

Philippians 2:17

What does Paul mean by "even if I am being poured out like a drink offering on the sacrifice and service coming from your faith"?

A drink offering was an Old Testament offering (a gift to God) of wine or water. Sometimes in the Old Testament, when animals were sacrificed, a drink offering was poured on top of the sacrifice. Paul is saying that the Philippians' joyful service of the Lord is like an Old Testament sacrifice. And if Paul dies for the sake of the gospel, it will be like a drink offering "poured on top" of their sacrifice.

Philippians 3:8

Why does Paul call his religious accomplishments "garbage"? What was the point of God's law in the Old Testament?

This is a complex issue that is dealt with in depth in Romans 1 – 11. The Old Testament law was never meant to make a person right with God. Rather, the law was intended to reveal our sin to us (and our great need of a Savior), to act as a restraint on sin, and to point us toward the life we're to live as believers.

Jesus doesn't abolish the Old Testament law; he fulfills it. And he fulfills different parts of it in different ways. For example:

- Sacrifices are no longer necessary, because Jesus is the perfect and final sacrifice.

- Food laws are no longer necessary, because Jesus' people show their distinctiveness by the holiness of their lives, rather than by the foods they eat.

- By contrast, Jesus deepens the moral requirements of the law. For example, it isn't just the act of murder which is sinful, but also being angry with your brother. It isn't just adultery which is wrong, but also lust and impure thoughts.

The Old Testament law can't produce the righteousness God requires, and that's why Paul describes attempts to use it in that way as "garbage" compared with the perfect righteousness available to us in Christ.

Philippians 3:10
What does it mean to know Christ?
Knowing Christ is about enjoying him, experiencing his power, and resembling him more and more. This is apparent in the four phrases Paul uses to describe what it means to know Christ in verses 10-11: he wants to know "the power of his resurrection" and "participation in his sufferings," "becoming like him in his death" and so "attaining to the resurrection from the dead."

Philippians 3:11
Why does Paul say "somehow"?
This is not Paul saying that he has doubts or is uncertain that he will be raised from the dead. He means that the exact path his life will take en route to that day is unclear to him.

Philippians 3:10-11
Why does Paul link the "participation of sharing in his sufferings" and "becoming like him in his death" with knowing Christ?
We tend to think that suffering and death are bad, and that resurrection and life are good. But Paul thinks that all these experiences are good because they help us to know Christ better – which is the greatest thing of all (3:8).

Philippians 3:15
Will all mature Christians believe exactly the same things?
This verse isn't saying that all mature Christians will always agree on everything – that won't be the case, at least not in this life. Instead, Paul is saying that all mature believers ought to live in the way he describes in Philippians 3:12-14, i.e. pressing on to become more like Christ. And he's confident (just as he is in 1:6) that if any of the Philippians are not yet at that stage, God will make this clear to them over time.

Philippians 4:7
What is "the peace of God, which transcends all understanding"?
People often read this verse and think that God will give them a feeling of peace. This may be true for some. But it is important to help young Christians understand the role of feelings, and to protect them from putting their trust in feelings rather than Jesus. Our feelings may change. Jesus Christ does not.

- Christians already have peace with God – the peace he has created between us and himself through Jesus (Romans 5:1). We were at war with God because of our sin. Now we are at peace because Jesus has taken the punishment for our sin.

- The fact that we are at peace with God means that we no longer need to be anxious. We can have "feelings of peace" because this peace truly exists.

- The peace we have with God is so wonderful that no one can fully understand or explain it.

"Transcends" can have a double meaning here. It can mean "beyond" in the sense of "we can't understand it." But it can also mean "better than" in the sense of "it is better than knowing all the answers."

Philippians 4:9

What does Paul mean when he says "the God of peace will be with you"?
The promise of verse 9 is plural – "The God of peace will be with you all."

Philippians 4:13

What does Paul mean when he says, "I can do all this through him who gives me strength"?
This doesn't mean God will give us strength to achieve anything we set our minds to doing. Paul means that God will give us the strength to be content in every situation.

Philippians 4:17

What does "credited to your account" mean?
This isn't a reference to earning salvation in some way, because Christ has earned salvation for us. Paul is referring to the individual reward that each believer will receive because of the good that he or she has done. See Matthew 5:12; 16:27; 25:20-23; Luke 19:15-19; Revelation 22:12.

FILM
SCRIPTS

Episode 1: Confident in Christ

Simo (Serbia): For Christians in the West, I wish you persecution. Then, you will know the sweetness of Christ.

You may think that I'm cruel, but I'm not. I wish you the best, and the best always comes from Christ.

Out of Christ is only death. In Christ is life.

[Philippians 1:1-11]

Barry: I grew up just outside London, in a town called Epsom. We used to go to a Methodist church which was directly across the street from where we lived. My dad would take us every single week; we never missed a Sunday. I don't think we missed a Sunday unless we were on holiday or something like that.

I stopped going when I was 16.

I went looking for it a few years back, and it had been demolished and replaced with an apartment block. But I remember what it was like. There was one group of people in the church who fell out with another group of people, and there were rumors and lots of gossip flying around. Even as a kid, I could pick up on it.

But the main reason that I stopped going was selfish really. As I think back, I just didn't love the people there. And it seemed liked too much effort to try.

—

When I start to read Paul's letter to the churches in Philippi, I find myself thinking, "This is a love letter." He never wrote like this to the churches in Corinth or Galatia: *"I long for all of you with the affection of Christ Jesus"* (Philippians 1:8).

And I wonder, how different would my church have looked if we'd loved each other like that, with the affection of Christ Jesus? Is that even possible?

—

This is the beginning of a journey into the heart of Philippians.

I want to find out how Paul was able to love like he loved. I want to know how he handled a church that was in danger of being poisoned by grumbling, arguing, and in-fighting. How he encouraged people to stand firm even in the face of frightening opposition.

I want to know how he was able to say, *"I have learned the secret of being content in any and every situation"* (Philippians 4:12), even when his life seemed desperately bleak. I want to know not just what I've been saved from, but what I've been saved for. And I want to meet real followers of Jesus all over the world who've put this ancient letter to the test.

—

I'm confident that Jesus Christ lived, died, was buried, was resurrected, and ascended, all so that I could be reconciled to God and enjoy him forever.

But here's the question: How can I be confident that I really am a Christian? How can I be confident that God is at work in my life? How can I know, for example, that at the end of my life, I'll still be a Christian?

—

Paul was extremely confident about the spiritual health of the people in Philippi:

"I always pray with joy because of your partnership in the gospel from the first day until now, being confident of this, that he who began a good work in you will carry it on to completion until the day of Christ Jesus." (Philippians 1:4-6)

—

How could he be so confident? Not because he was confident in them, but because he was confident in Christ.

Remarkably, for a man who was in chains and under house arrest in Rome as he wrote this letter, Paul was convinced, absolutely convinced, that God is in control. Not just when things were going according to Paul's plan, but also when they weren't.

He knew this, not just from Scripture – he knew it from his own experience. This was the place, about 20 years or so after Jesus was crucified, that four men came and preached the gospel in Europe for the first time. There was the apostle Paul, there was a young evangelist called Timothy, there was a church leader called Silas, and a medical doctor and historian called Luke.

Initially, they hadn't planned to come here at all. Originally, they were planning to head into Asia, but God had other ideas.

The book of Acts says they were kept from preaching there, and they were also prevented from carrying out their plan B, which was to travel into Bithynia. So they ended up spending the night in Troas, where Paul had this vision of a Macedonian man begging for help.

And one of the leading cities in Macedonia was Philippi.

—

I don't know about you, but I sometimes remember those moments when I longed for something that I didn't get, or I remember a time when I got something that I really didn't want. And if you're not careful, it can cripple you with regret.

But Paul understood a life-saving truth. He knew that when things don't pan out as we hope, it's because God in his goodness has other ideas. In Christ, thwarted plans are the beginning of something better.

As these new believers in Philippi well knew! If things had gone the way Paul originally wanted, they might never have heard the gospel.

Sometimes what I want is actually the very worst thing that God could give me. One pastor put it like this: "God gives us exactly what we would ask for if we knew everything that he knows."

Simo: I was in prison, and there in prison I preached to 80 prisoners who, after they finished their sentence in prison, they came to my home. Everybody took a parcel of literature, in Albanian, and after that, it led to 40 churches in Kosovo and hundreds in Albania.

Barry: Our loving Father is utterly in control. Every drop of rain finds its appointed target, and that means that nothing's accidental or haphazard.

Even the greatest evil in all of history, the murder of God's Son, achieved the greatest possible good: the salvation of everyone who believes in him.

When God intends to do something, nothing can stop him. As Paul says, "He who began a good work in you will carry it on to completion" (Philippians 1:6). What God starts, he finishes.

—

But how can we know that God has started to work in us? Well, the clue is in Paul's phrase, "partnership in the gospel."

It's not just that they believed the gospel. They'd been living it out.

You can see that from the story of Lydia in Acts chapter 16. She was a business-woman, one of the first people in Philippi to become a follower of Jesus. After she believes the gospel, she immediately starts living it out by inviting Paul and his companions to stay at her home.

It's the same with the jailer who threw Paul and Silas into a Philippian prison. As soon as the jailer believes the gospel, he starts living it out. He washes Paul's wounds, he gets baptized, he invites them into his home, and gives them a meal. His emotions changed too. We read that he was filled with joy.

That's how you know a person is in Christ. The love they receive from Jesus starts overflowing to others. First of all, it overflows to fellow believers. If someone had said to Paul that they loved Jesus but preferred not to get involved with their local church, he would have had little confidence that they knew Christ at all.

When God really is at work in us, our attitude toward other people changes.

But if God always finishes the work he starts, why should we bother doing anything? Doesn't that just take away all our responsibility?

Well, actually Paul says it's because God is at work in you, that you have a responsibility to respond. Listen to the way he prays for them:

"This is my prayer: that your love may abound more and more in knowledge and depth of insight..." (Philippians 1:9)

He wants them to be deliberate and intentional about growing in their knowledge and depth of insight. For us, at the very least, that means doing whatever we can to get to know God's word better.

"... so that you may be able to discern what is best, and may be pure and blameless for the day of Christ, filled with the fruit of righteousness that comes through Jesus Christ – to the glory and praise of God." (Philippians 1:10-11)

The uncomfortable reality is that we don't always know "what is best."

Things that seem good and feel right can be disastrous for us. That's a real challenge: are we willing to keep growing in our knowledge of God's word and follow it wherever it leads, even if it goes somewhere difficult or uncomfortable?

Lenny (USA): For me, being a pastor, everything that I preach, it deals with me first.

Every time I'm reading something in the Bible and it's a particular subject, if I'm preaching on grace, the things that I get in that "sermon," it starts with me first. There's lots of times where I'm like, "Dang, God, you're saying this?" It's like "gut check."

If I'm uncomfortable, I've got to change something. The Bible should hurt. It's going to hurt. The gospel hurts. It's going to be offensive, but that's because you need to do some dying. You need to do some changing.

Barbara (Rwanda): When I got saved, the pastor told us that you read Matthew to Revelation. That's the first introduction. Everyone goes to Matthew. It's later, when you mature in some sense, that you

go to the Old Testament and read the prophecies about him and all. But you get introduced to Christ and the Bible in Matthew.

Who is this man who was born of a virgin? What does the Bible say about him? He came to save us.

I do believe if you want to know Christ, go to the Bible.

Barry: When I was a small child, crossing a busy street with my father, if I was the one choosing to hold his hand, then he knew I could let go of it anytime I wanted, and I probably would.

But because he was the one choosing to hold my hand, I knew he'd never let me go. He loved me too much. Like Jesus said, *"No one can snatch them out of my Father's hand"* (John 10:29). We can be confident that God will finish what he starts.

—

Scripture tells us in Colossians, chapter one, that God the Son never had a beginning. He has always existed.

Scripture tells us in Ephesians, chapter one, that his love for those who are in him never had a beginning either. His love has always existed.

Because that love never had a beginning, it can never have an end.

It's the greatest love you've ever known.

Episode 2: Living in Christ

Simo (Serbia): Before I became a Christian, for me, life was work. Tireless work.

[Philippians 1:12-26]

Barry: For me, for a long time, I lived for... and I'm not proud of this... but I lived for girlfriends and academic achievement. Those were the two big things. When I didn't have those things, I just felt worthless. I felt like I wasn't lovable. I felt like I wasn't a worthwhile human being. I felt invisible. To be honest, I felt miserable.

—

What about you? What are you living for?

Well, here's one way of finding out. Ask yourself this question. What is the one thing, if it was taken from you, would make you feel like life wasn't worth living?

—

Something you can't miss as you read this section of Philippians, and actually the whole letter, is Paul's joy. Now as he's writing, he's under house arrest in Rome, chained to a Roman guard day and night, knowing that at any moment, the order for his execution might come. Yet, he keeps telling them how joyful he is.

Now I don't know what you're struggling with at this point in your life. It could be problems with your marriage, problems in singleness, at work, perhaps persecution for being a Christian. But if Paul can be joyful in his circumstances, then surely there can be hope for us in our circumstances too.

Since Paul became a follower of Jesus, just about everything had been taken from him.

—

The most recent report from the organization *Open Doors* says that Christians worldwide are facing the worst levels of persecution in modern times. At a conservative estimate, the number of people currently facing persecution for following Jesus stands at 215 million.

Simo: And even when I came here, after ten years, they threw stones at my windows. I couldn't sleep at night. Just in the middle of the night, one o'clock, two o'clock...

I was persecuted. I was almost every week at the police station. They were visiting my home very often. I was in prison for one month because of distribution of literature.

Barry: Amazingly, with all of his hardship, Paul says, *"I rejoice ... and I will continue to rejoice"* (Philippians 1:18). What's the secret to Paul's joy?

The author C.S. Lewis said, "Don't let your happiness depend on something you may lose." So what does your happiness depend on? Comfort? Money? Sex? The approval of others? Family? These aren't necessarily bad things, but they are fragile things. When they go, they'll take your happiness with them. The secret of Paul's joy is that he's living for something else, something glorious that can't die or be damaged or be taken away.

"For to me," he says, *"to live is Christ"* (Philippians 1:21). He finds his deepest

happiness in Christ, and because he knows Christ is in control of all that happens to him, turning everything for good, all his circumstances are cause for rejoicing. Not even his chains can depress him, because they've served to advance the gospel.

Because of his chains, a constant stream of high-ranking, hard-nosed, thoroughly pagan Roman guards have been shackled, one after the other, to one of the most persuasive evangelists who ever lived. So the whole palace guard are hearing about Christ.

And that's emboldened others to proclaim the gospel without fear. And even if there are jealous Christians trying to stir up trouble for Paul while he's in chains, they're preaching the gospel in order to do that. So Paul says:

"What does it matter? The important thing is that in every way, whether from false motives or true, Christ is preached. And because of this I rejoice." (Philippians 1:18)

The way to know joy in every circumstance is to know that Jesus is in every circumstance.

Paul saw the fingerprints of God everywhere, even on his chains.

—

[Map showing the growth of Christianity over time appears here. Note that the map is intended to show only where the gospel has been preached, and where churches have been established.]

What Paul couldn't have foreseen is this. At the start of the fourth century,

the Roman Empire launched a sustained effort to crush Christianity completely.

But by the end of the century, even the emperors themselves were followers of Christ.

—

So, to live is Christ, but Paul doesn't stop there. He says, *"to die is gain"* (Philippians 1:21). Now how can death be a gain? Of course, he doesn't say this lightly. The threat of death is constantly over him. He's got no idea when he's going to be called to present his case before the authorities. His life might be over in an hour.

But Christ is more than a way of life to Paul. Christ is a way of death too. Paul knows that even if he dies, all that will happen is that he'll be reunited with his greatest treasure, his greatest happiness.

That will make you radical. Radically fearless, radically loving! If Christ is the one who gives you most joy – not money, or family, or sex, or comfort, or status, or freedom from prison – if Christ is the one who gives you the most joy, then nothing can rob you of that joy. Suffering and death become your servants. All they can do is usher you into the presence of your deepest joy.

To live is Christ, and to die is gain.

Simo: I knew if they kill me, I go to heaven. I was not afraid. There is a text in the Bible, that Jesus died on the cross to deliver us from the bondage of fear of death.

Barry: Would you go so far as to say you were joyful in the middle of that?

Simo: Yes, I was really joyful. I was so happy.

Barry: Why were you happy?

Simo: Because I knew, I felt Christ's presence with me all the time. He was just near me.

—

Barry: But if we're honest, Jesus isn't our greatest treasure. So, we miss the secret of joy.

If we're honest, we would rewrite that sentence:

"For me, to live is having friends and family around me, and to die is loss."

"For me, to live is being comfortable and avoiding all suffering, and to die is loss."

"For me, to live is enjoying my freedom, and to die is being confined to a small, wooden box in the ground."

So here's the challenge. If your closest friend, the person who knows you best, were to finish that sentence for you, what would they say? For you, to live is... what? What is the one thing, if it were taken from you, would make you feel like life wasn't worth living?

There is only one way of living that death cannot steal from you, and that is to live for Christ.

Because when death comes, it will only succeed in bringing you face to face with your greatest joy, face to face with the one who died and was raised from death so that you could join him in a place where death and suffering no longer have any claim on you. Face to face with the one who knows the very worst about you, yet loves you the very best.

For to me, to live is Christ and to die is gain.

Episode 3: One in Christ

Basma (Jordan): They [ISIS] failed, definitely they failed. Because they did not expect that these large numbers would hold on to their faith.

[Philippians 1:27 – 2:11]

Barry: How do you get along with everyone at your church? Is there anyone you try and avoid? Anyone you're jealous of? Is there competition for power, information, recognition?

You can hear Paul's concern for unity all over Philippians, but especially in this part of the letter. He says, *"Stand firm in the one Spirit"* – that is the Holy Spirit given to all believers – *"striving together as one ... being like-minded ... being one in spirit and of one mind"* (Philippians 1:27, 2:2).

He repeatedly uses this Greek word, *koinonia*. It's a word that means fellowship, participation, partnership, oneness. Now, why should this togetherness matter so much?

—

We don't always think of evangelism as a communal activity, but there's a particularly convincing kind of evangelism that can only be done communally.

Jesus said, *"By this everyone will know*

that you are my disciples, if you love one another" (John 13:35).

When we genuinely love each other in our local churches across lines of race, gender, and age, it shows that we really are followers of Jesus. It also shows a watching world that the gospel is credible and powerful.

—

But this kind of unity is constantly under threat. One threat to our togetherness is opposition. Just think about what happened to the disciples when Jesus was arrested. They scattered. That's why Paul tells us to stand as one without being frightened in any way by those who oppose you.

First, the opposition of these people shows they're set against God, which means ultimately they will lose; and second, their opposition confirms that you really do belong to Christ because your opponents have seen in you something of him.

Now, we rightly celebrate the fact that our faith in Christ is a wonderful gift from God, but here in Philippians Paul says there's another gift God gives, and it's one we might prefer not to unwrap.

Paul knew they were facing serious opposition and yet he says this:

"It has been granted to you on behalf of Christ not only to believe in him, but also to suffer for him" (Philippians 1:29).

How can suffering for Christ be a gift?

In the book of Hebrews, it says, *"Endure hardship as discipline"* (Hebrews 12:7). Now, when you see a man disciplining his child, you assume he's the dad. The child is his son or daughter. Well, that's exactly the biblical logic: when you suffer for Christ, it's a gift, because it shows that you're in this incredibly privileged relationship with almighty God. He's your Father.

Also, if you're his child, that means you're his heir. Do you realize that one day soon you'll inherit all that is his?

Listen to what Paul says in his letter to the Christians in Rome:

"Now if we are children, then we are heirs – heirs of God and co-heirs with Christ, if indeed we share in his sufferings in order that we may also share in his glory." (Romans 8:17)

As Paul well knew, the discipline of suffering and hardship is never pleasant, but it always has a purpose – to make you more and more like Jesus so that you will one day share in his glory.

Basma: There are moments when I think about how our honor was insulted, we were humiliated, and we were displaced. I think of all of the insults and persecution I have been faced with.

But I still think back and compare the insults we had and what Jesus had to endure by his enemies, what he went through, the bitterness, betrayal and the condemnation... ours was nothing compared to his.

Nashwan (Jordan): People came to the

conviction that money and property is of no use. It does not help. The only thing that is beneficial is the Lord Almighty. Nothing else will save them. Nothing.

Barry: Opposition can threaten the unity of our churches but there's another threat and it's much closer to home. The theologian Augustine called it the mother of all sins: pride.

It makes us want to compare ourselves with others. It makes us jealous when our friends do well. It keeps us from asking for help or admitting our faults. It drives our demand for recognition and applause, and makes us depressed and bitter when we don't get it. It makes us cling to our low self-esteem and use that as an excuse for self-pity. It makes us blame everyone else when things go wrong.

And it was bubbling just under the surface of the Philippian church, threatening their oneness in Christ.

That's why, after telling them to be one in spirit and of one mind, Paul says, "*Do nothing out of selfish ambition or vain conceit.*"

He says, "*In humility, value others above yourselves, not looking to your own interests but each of you to the interests of the others*" (Philippians 2:3-4).

It's only when we stand alongside real humility that we're shocked out of ourselves and begin to see just how full of pride we are by comparison. That's what Paul does for us here as he stands us alongside this stunning portrait of Jesus.

"*In your relationships with one another,*
have the same mindset as Christ Jesus:
Who, being in very nature God, did not
consider equality with God something to
be used to his own advantage; rather, he
made himself nothing…*" (Philippians 2:5-7)

—

"*Being in very nature God … made himself
nothing.*" Imagine that. You gaze into the very heart of the Creator of the universe and what do you see? There's not a trace of conceit. There's no lust for power, no desire to exploit – just pure humility.

—

But it wasn't just that Jesus made himself nothing. He took "*the very nature of a servant … made in human likeness*" (Philippians 2:7). Now, the word translated "servant" there is actually *doulos*, which means "slave" – someone who's got no rights whatsoever.

Ironically, it's the word Paul used right at the start of the letter, where he described himself as a servant, a "slave," of Christ. And yet here is Christ – and he makes himself a slave to all mankind.

It shatters all our pretension, all our pride: the Son of God, the One who created human beings in the first place, becomes a human being himself so that he can give up his rights and become like a slave. Someone put it like this: "No one has ever descended so low because no one has ever come from so high."

—

But it wasn't just that he became a slave. "*He humbled himself by becoming obedient to death – even death on a cross*" (Philippians 2:8). God the Son chose to live a slave's life, and then die a slave's death.

Shamed, spat upon, scourged, stripped naked, and then publicly nailed to a piece of wood in the company of common criminals. If you really want to be "God-like" in this life – this is what it looks like.

And Paul's saying it's only this kind of humility that can make us truly united with each other in our churches.

I think about the church I struggled with as a boy. What would it have looked like if I'd gone each week with that picture of Christ in my mind?

Nashwan: It is hard to express how I feel about what Jesus Christ did for us. There is no description. The Lord became a man, was crucified, tortured – all this to forgive our sins.

There are no words that can adequately describe what he did.

Barry: Paul then tells us the result of Jesus' humility and suffering:

"Therefore God exalted him to the highest place and gave him the name that is above every name, that at the name of Jesus every knee should bow, in heaven and on earth and under the earth, and every tongue acknowledge that Jesus Christ is Lord, to the glory of God the Father." (Philippians 2:9-11)

—

One day, Jesus will be publicly exalted, having been publicly shamed. And if we stand firm, even if we are publicly shamed, we too will be exalted.

—

One of the most telling clues about

whether we really do love Christ is that we start to love the people that Christ loves. When he draws people to himself, he draws them toward each other.

—

You know, if I'm honest, I find it's the easiest thing in the world to talk generally about standing firm in the one spirit or striving together as one for the faith of the gospel. It's all a bit vague. It's like world peace – everyone says they're in favor of it.

But the kind of love and unity that Paul is talking about here is very deliberate, very self-sacrificial. It actually costs us something.

He's talking about the kind of love and unity that commits day by day to the same specific local body of believers, standing firm with them, striving together with them, with all of their weirdness, and their struggles, and their rough edges.

For the most part, that was the story of the believers in Philippi. And the question is – is it our story too?

Episode 4: Obedient in Christ

Antoine (Rwanda): I used to tell people, "I too used to speak like that, but now my life has changed. You too need to change."

That kind of thing encourages you, because you know the gospel we are preaching is a life-transforming gospel.

[Philippians 2:12-30]

Barry: If all my sins are forgiven by God

because of what Jesus has done on the cross, then does it really matter how I live now? Won't God forgive me anyway?

Paul begins this section of his letter with a "therefore," which means that everything he's about to say is built on what's gone before. What he's just shown us, of course, is that stunning picture of Jesus – how Christ showed his obedience to God the Father by humbling himself, making himself a servant, and becoming obedient to death, even death on a cross.

Now Paul makes this connection between Christ and the Christian: just as Jesus obeyed his Father, so we must obey our Father too.

—

I love the precious truth that there's nothing we can do to earn salvation. It's a gift freely given. I'm fully accepted by God, loved as dearly as he loves his Son, made a co-heir with Christ, solely on the basis of Christ's obedience, and not my obedience.

But here's the danger. We can start to think, "If I'm accepted by God on the basis of Christ's obedience, then my obedience doesn't matter." Of course, we probably wouldn't say that out loud, but subconsciously we think, "I can live my life however I want, because whatever happens, I'm saved. I'm going to heaven."

But Paul's saying, "Your obedience is absolutely crucial." If there's little Christian obedience in our lives, it's possible we're not Christian at all. One person put it like this: "Religion says, 'I obey, therefore I'm accepted.' Christianity says, 'I'm accepted, therefore I obey.'"

If I'm consistently not obeying, there's a good chance that I wasn't actually accepted by God in the first place. That's what Paul means by *"work out your salvation"* (Philippians 2:12). It means keep acting in line with your salvation. Be obedient to Christ.

—

I always thought I was a Christian, but it wasn't until 1992 that I knew I really was. The difference really was the attitude that I had toward obedience.

Before that, obedience was something I just had to do, even if I didn't want to, which was most of the time. I was like a spoiled child who was only obedient to his parents because he thinks he can earn himself some extra pocket money, not out of any love for them – just sheer joyless, loveless duty.

Then, in Easter 1992, something really strange happened. I still can't account for it in non-supernatural terms. Almost overnight it was – middle of my first year at university – I suddenly found that I wanted to be obedient to God because I felt love for him, and I wanted to do everything I could to be more like him.

Also, because I began to see and feel that living in that way was good. It was true. It led to happiness – if not always in the short term, certainly in the longer term.

That was the point in my life I think when I really started to work out my salvation. That was the moment when I really began to see the beauty of Christ.

—

How important one word can be. Paul doesn't say, "Work *for* your salvation." He says, "Work *out* your salvation."

We can't work *for* our salvation because it's already been won for us by Christ. But once we know that salvation, it begins to work itself out in loads of ways: in our relationships, the way we relate to the people in our church, in our marriages, the way we express our sexuality, our parenting, at work, in the way we talk, the way we spend our money and our time.

—

And we're to live out our salvation with fear and trembling, with the consciousness that nothing we do is hidden from God. I think it's really telling that Paul mentions that they ought to be obedient not just when he's with them, but also when he's absent from them.

The temptation, of course, is to obey only when other people are watching, hoping they notice the good things we're doing, especially church leaders like Paul. What does our obedience look like when only God is watching?

—

But now there's a real curve ball. Read the end of that sentence. Paul says:

"Work out your salvation with fear and trembling, for it is God who works in you to will and to act in order to fulfil his good purpose." (Philippians 2:12-13)

Well, which is it? Are we the ones working out our salvation? Or is God doing it?

As I discovered back in 1992, it's only God who can work in us so that we have this desire and the power to act obediently. That is something that is supernatural.

But then, of course, when all is said and done, we must act. Paul wouldn't bother to say any of this if our obedience just happened automatically. We have to act on the godly desires that God has planted in us.

—

There's incredible beauty in obedience to Christ.

I remember once having lunch with a man who had had a wonderful lifelong ministry of preaching, pastoring, writing. I guess many would have said that he was the spiritual giant of his generation. All I wanted to do was just ply him with questions.

And I've never forgotten this. For the entire lunch, all he wanted to do was talk to me about what was going on in my life. He seemed genuinely concerned for my welfare and he barely said anything about himself. It was as if he'd forgotten who he was.

He was one of the most joyful men I've ever met, and I'm sure that was precisely because he was also one of the most self-forgetful.

Barbara (Rwanda): Her name was Nicole – Nicole Kalisa. She was one of the leaders of the youth group. The thing that really touched me about her character is the brokenness she had as a Christian, and the faith, the belief, that she had in the Scriptures. It was so real and so practical with her. It wasn't just another trend. She was very genuine. She was young, probably four or five years older than I was, but you could feel it was real. Christ in her was real.

She imparted that to me in those early

ages. She made Christ look like a friend. She made the Holy Spirit look like someone you could talk with, like I'm talking to you. It was so real.

Barry: Paul says that when we live like this, we'll shine in the world like stars in the sky. We'll be a luminous, attractive presence in the places where we live.

But one of the big threats to our "shining" is something that might seem pretty innocuous. He says, make sure you *"do everything without grumbling or arguing"* (Philippians 2:14).

This is something we see earlier in the letter: our good witness to the world depends upon our love for each other as believers in the local church. When we grumble and argue, it makes the gospel less believable to those who are watching.

It also says something about our view of God. It's an expression of mistrust in God's wise arrangement of all our circumstances. It forgets his infinite goodness to us. And against the backdrop of Jesus' humility and servant-heartedness, grumbling and arguing just seem completely out of place.

—

I love the story told by the eighteenth-century pastor John Newton. It's a brilliant illustration of how foolish grumbling is.

He says, "Suppose a man was going to New York to take possession of a huge inheritance. On the way, his carriage breaks down just a mile before he gets to the city, which means that he's got to walk the rest of the way.

What would we think of that man if we saw that man walking the last mile whining and complaining, "My carriage is broken down. I'm going to have to get new wheels!"

It really should be very hard for us to grumble when we remember who we are and where we're going.

—

And Paul tells us who we are. We are children of God, adopted into his family, about to claim our inheritance.

What a difference it would make to our happiness if we actually took God at his word and believed that.

—

So how do we make sure we become blameless and pure? How can we shine like stars, according to Paul? By holding firmly to the word of life, the gospel of Jesus Christ.

You might have heard the old phrase: "Preach the gospel – if necessary, use words." It's the idea that really you don't need to verbally share the gospel with others. You just need to live a good life and that will be enough to win people over.

But the thing about authentic disciples of Jesus is that they want to make disciples of others too. Part of holding firmly to the word of life will be holding out the word of life to others.

Although, to be honest, we sometimes struggle with what to say when we're talking about Jesus. It doesn't always go according to plan.

Antoine: When you are a pastor, you preach in a church, so people who come to church, they are already receptive. But when you preach in the market, and I did that so many times – preach in the market, preach on the street, preach on the bus – that's where you get people who are hostile.

They say, "Why are you making so much noise here? Why are you telling us that? Why are you imposing on us your faith?"

Now that I'm a pastor, or when you preach as a pastor, people will say, "Oh fine, he's a pastor! What else do you expect from a pastor?" It's a bit different from the past.

But actually, the essential thing is not how people react when you preach. Because you are sowing seeds. You don't know when those seeds are going to sprout out and bear fruit, so you don't worry about that.

Barry: How will I know what to say? That's often the big question we have about evangelism.

But, as Jesus says in Luke 6:45, *"The mouth speaks what the heart is full of."* So, if you want to speak about Jesus more naturally and more frequently, make your heart full of him – and then speak out of the overflow of that passion.

How do we do that? Paul would say, "Go to the word of life, God's word, because it will make you passionate about Christ."

As we listen to Scripture and fill our hearts more and more with the goodness of Christ, just naturally we'll want to start sharing that goodness with other people, whether they're Christian or not. We'll start to do what Jesus called us to do when he said, *"Go and make disciples of all nations"* (Matthew 28:19). We'll start to become what we must all be: disciple-making disciples.

—

So what does it actually look like to work out your salvation? A real-life example would be helpful at this point, and Paul gives us two.

Timothy had helped to plant the church in Philippi. Paul describes him as having *"served with me in the work of the gospel,"* *"as a son with his father."* *"I have no one else like him,"* he says, *"who will show genuine concern for your welfare"* (Philippians 2:22 and 20).

And Epaphroditus is the man the Philippians sent to Paul to take care of him while he was in chains: his *"brother, co-worker, and fellow soldier"* (Philippians 2:25).

In fact, Epaphroditus had taken a journey of many hundreds of miles over many weeks just so that he could take care of Paul's needs. Apparently, he was ill and almost died, and yet still he longs to make the return journey back to Philippi, bearing Paul's letter.

"Honor people like him," Paul says (v 30), "because they love others. Even if it means risking their lives."

—

So when people look at us, I wonder what they see? Can they see distinctive, loving people, eager to obey Jesus and tell others about him whatever the cost?

Can they see people like Timothy and Epaphroditus, who even now, as we read about them 2,000 years on, shine like stars in the sky?

Episode 5: Righteous in Christ

Prasoon (India): I grew up in a religion which is cyclical, so you are born and you live a life, and then you are reborn, and as long as you continue to do good works – in society, at home, with other individuals – you can become right with God.

That was the concept that I had, to become right with God. Basically through "karma-marga," through good works. That's the path I followed.

[Philippians 3:1-9]

Barry: What are you doing to try and make God accept you?

—

Religion is spelled D-O. Christianity is spelled D-O-N-E. Religions say that God will accept me because of the good things that I do. Christianity says that God will accept me because of what Christ has done. And when we get the two confused, it's spiritually devastating.

—

In a survey not so long ago, they asked 7,000 churchgoers whether they agreed with this statement: "The way to be accepted by God is to try sincerely to live a good life." More than 60% agreed with that statement.

In other words, many Christians think that they can be good enough for God by doing good things, or not doing bad things.

For some people it means doing a lot of religious things, like going to church, or communion, or confession.

—

That was very much the case for Paul before he met Jesus. In this part of his letter, Paul gives us his résumé, his spiritual CV as a Jewish man, and it really is exceptional:

"… circumcised on the eighth day, of the people of Israel, of the tribe of Benjamin, a Hebrew of Hebrews; in regard to the law, a Pharisee; as for zeal, persecuting the church; as for righteousness based on the law, faultless." (Philippians 3:5-6)

He came from the right kind of family. He was descended from God's chosen people, the people of Israel. He joined a hugely respected Jewish order known for their hyper-strict adherence to the religious laws. He was a Hebrew of Hebrews, a leader of men, highly educated. If there were moral laws to be kept, he sincerely kept them. Religiously and ethically, he'd done everything right.

And here's the word that Paul uses to describe that mountain of moral and religious achievement: "garbage."

—

In the original Greek, the work translated "garbage" is much stronger. If you could smell what you're seeing right now, you'd get an idea of the word Paul has in mind. Now, how can all that moral and religious righteousness suddenly seem like excrement to him?

Because now that he knows Jesus, he sees what righteousness really looks like, and it makes his own so-called "righteousness" look disgusting by comparison. He understands that what he needs is a righteousness that is not his own, but comes from God.

All the things he thought were so powerful in making him acceptable were useless, fit only to be thrown out. *"I consider them garbage,"* says Paul, *"that I may gain Christ and be found in him"* (Philippians 3:8-9).

He knows that at the end of his life, when he stands before God and God says, "Why should I accept you?" Paul will hand him his résumé and on it will be one word: "Jesus."

—

If you're tempted to think there's anything on your résumé or your CV, anything you've done that can make you acceptable to God, Paul has two words for you: "Watch out."

He said the same thing to the young Christians in Philippi. They were being told by some very respectable, very credible, very religious people who actually claimed to be Christian – they were being told that they could never be acceptable to God unless they got themselves circumcised.

He calls these people "dogs" – stray animals leading others astray, spreading a dangerous and potentially fatal disease.

These "dogs" were insisting that Jesus is all well and good, but you need something else as well: you need to be circumcised.

And though, for most of us, circumcision isn't the issue anymore, the dogs are not dead. They're still out there – or in here – trying to bully us into thinking that Jesus' righteousness doesn't go far enough, that we somehow have to meet him halfway with our own righteousness.

With our churchgoing, our money-giving, our communion-taking, our Bible-reading, our doing of good deeds.

It's not that any of these things are bad. They're wonderful things to do.

But they become bad if I start to think they can make me righteous – if they start to take the place of my dependency on Jesus and his righteousness.

We need to repent, not only of our sin, but also of our righteousness.

—

Can you see that our own attempt at righteousness is like garbage next to the righteousness of Jesus? In fact, it's worse than that. It's more like toxic waste.

If we're trying to make ourselves righteous by our own efforts, we'll either become self-righteous or self-loathing. On the one hand, if I believe I can make myself righteous, and I think I'm doing a great job of it, then I'll just get proud and I'll start to look down on people. On the other hand, if I'm doing a bad job, then I'll get totally depressed because no matter how hard I try, I keep failing.

Prasoon: I think, emotionally, I waver between these two. There were times when I would do good, so-called "good works," and I would feel proud that I was able to do these things, and perhaps my parents are happy, others are happy. I can relate to God now.

But there were times when I didn't do those things. I felt so guilty. And I thought, I have not achieved the mark and I need to strive hard in order to please God.

Barry: The worst part of it is this:

If I'm trying to make myself righteous, I'm effectively saying to God, "I've done all these things for you, so now you owe me." It's absurd. I'm treating the Creator of the universe as if he's in my debt. When we do that, we insult and belittle him. We're obeying him to get what we want, rather than obeying him simply because we love him.

Isn't it amazing how we can use absolutely anything, even our good deeds, to treat God with contempt? We need to repent, not only of our sin, but also of our righteousness.

We badly need the righteousness of Jesus.

—

As Paul says, we should put no confidence in the flesh. In other words, we should put no confidence in who we are or what we've done, whether it be circumcision or any other moral or religious act. Our confidence should be solely in Christ and what he has done.

—

Now, of course, this is a controversial claim in this day and age. But Jesus is the only one who can make us good enough for God.

Why? Because he, and he alone, lived the life we should have lived. And then he, and he alone, died the death we deserved to die. All so that we could be accepted by God and enjoy him forever.

Where else on earth can you find righteousness like that? Our righteousness must be in him and only in him.

—

John Bunyan, who wrote *The Pilgrim's Progress*, and who himself spent many years in prison, was walking in the fields one morning and this line came into his mind: "Your righteousness is in heaven."

Bunyan said, "With the eyes of my soul, I saw Jesus at the Father's right hand so that wherever I was or whatever I was doing, God could not say to me, 'Where is your righteousness?' for it is always right before him."

"I saw," said Bunyan, "that it is not my good frame of heart that made my righteousness better, or my bad frame that made my righteousness worse, for my righteousness is Christ."

—

The only way we get his righteousness is not by moral or religious efforts, but by simple trust in him. It is a righteousness that comes from God on the basis of faith.

Prasoon: It is only by grace alone through faith alone and in Christ alone I'm accepted before God. My good day at work, my alms-giving, even my ministry doesn't make me feel good in front of God. It's only the work of Christ, and only Christ's atoning work on the cross.

This is something that I keep reminding myself of. Somebody said that we need to be preaching the gospel to ourselves daily. This is something that I keep reminding myself of, that my identity does not come from what I do. My identity rests in Christ alone.

Barry: If anyone in the history of the world could appeal to God on the basis of his moral or religious goodness, Paul was the man. But he doesn't do that anymore because all of it, says Paul, all of it is garbage compared to the surpassing worth of knowing Christ Jesus.

Our hearts are always trying to pull us off track here, even if we've been Christians for a long time. We can so easily start relating to God through our own credentials, through our own résumé, rather than through Christ. Sometimes even our attempts at obedience can be a subtle way of seeking to be our own savior. We need to watch out.

We may not be putting our confidence in circumcision, but have we started putting our confidence in circumstances, our education, our family, our status symbols, our moral decency?

Or have we started putting our confidence in religious things to make us righteous? Things like baptism or speaking in tongues or saying our prayers or reading our Bibles or going to church or telling others about Jesus?

And here's how you know if you're putting your confidence in Christ's righteousness or your own:

On an occasion when you've disobeyed Christ in some way, do you think you're less of a Christian than you were before?

When someone asks you, "Are you a Christian?" do you answer, "Yes, but not a very good one."

In a week when you've read your Bible, been to church, and told someone about Christ, are you more acceptable to God?

—

If you answered yes to any of those questions, then you've not understood that your righteousness depends entirely on Christ's righteousness.

On an occasion when you've disobeyed Christ in some way, do you think you're less of a Christian than you were before?

No, because Christ is your righteousness.

When someone asks you, "Are you a Christian?" do you answer, "Yes, but not a very good one."

No, because Christ is your righteousness.

In a week when you've read your Bible, been to church, and told someone about Christ, are you more acceptable to God?

No, because Christ is your righteousness.

Christ is your righteousness.

Episode 6: Transformed in Christ

Lenny (USA): It wasn't until I was 19 or 20, when God seriously got a hold of my life, that my outlook of the police changed. When you have these young black males who have never had a good experience with the police, it's hard for them to erase that bad experience. First impressions – they last.

Barry: When you became a Christian, how did that impact the way you saw what was going on with the police?

Lenny: It boils down to "love." Because the gospel should change you. The gospel should change every single thing about you.

[Philippians 3:10-21]

Barry: There was a time when Jesus took his disciples aside and talked to them about the kingdom of heaven.

"The kingdom of heaven is like treasure hidden in a field. When a man found it, he hid it again, and then in his joy went and sold all he had and bought that field.

"Again, the kingdom of heaven is like a merchant looking for fine pearls. When he found one of great value, he went away and sold everything he had and bought it." (Matthew 13:44-46)

I can just imagine the response I'd get if I told my wife I'd sold literally everything we have in order to buy one thing. But what if you knew that that one thing was infinitely more precious than everything else you have put together. That was Paul's story.

Paul describes his mountain of moral, religious, and ethical achievement as "garbage" next to the surpassing worth of knowing Jesus. Like the man who knew he's found the greatest treasure on earth, Paul thought nothing of sacrificing everything he had to get more of him [Jesus].

That's the theme of this part of the letter. Jesus is so valuable to Paul, creates so much joy in him, that he'll do whatever it takes to know Jesus better and become more like him. He says, *"I want to know Christ"* (Philippians 3:10).

—

How do we become more like Christ? According to Paul, one of the ways we do that is by imitating others.

But this is strange. Here's a man who said, "May I never boast except in the cross" (Galatians 6:14). Yet here he is in verse 17 saying, *"Join together in following my example."* He wants the Philippians to copy him. Isn't that a little egocentric?

When Jesus called me to follow him back in 1992, I didn't hear any audible voices telling me what to do. I didn't have any visions of Jesus or anything like that. I certainly didn't know my Bible very well either. But what I did have was an incredible example of what being a Christian looks like.

He was a student worker in a church in Oxford, England, and he would meet with me every week or so to read the Bible with me. We'd read a few paragraphs. He'd ask the same basic questions. "What does this tell us about God? What does this tell us about us? What should we do about it?"

Then he just prayed with me. But what really left an impression on me, and what still does as I think about it, was this man's life and character, his good humor, his kindness toward me, his patience with me, the fact that he prayed for me every time we met, his love of Scripture. He didn't have to ask me to do those things myself. You couldn't help but want to imitate him.

Rafael (Peru): See, there was a professor that discipled me. Yes, he was a humble person, happy, but in serious issues he was always wanting to do things right, and I felt like he was a mentor that would help me with anything I needed. He truly was like Jesus – he had a lot of love and passion for souls.

Barry: The teaching that really sticks is the teaching that we see lived out in the life of someone else. That's why Paul says, *"Follow my example"* and *"keep your eyes on those who live as we do"* (Philippians 3:17). This was especially important for the Philippians because, at this point, they didn't even have a New Testament to learn from. What they did have was the life and character of the man who was about to write half of it.

For me, that's another reason why being committed to a good local church is so crucial. It's where you find the most godly people to imitate, but it's also the place where you yourself can be an example to others.

—

There's something else that can make us more like Christ: suffering.

We've become so good at hiding suffering and death that we're more frightened of them than we've ever been, but Paul embraces them.

"I want to know Christ – yes, to know the power of his resurrection and participation in his sufferings, becoming like him in his death, and so, somehow, attaining to the resurrection from the dead." (Philippians 3:10-11)

—

This is shocking to many of us, that Paul would long to participate in suffering for Christ. It certainly wasn't something that he sought out for its own sake, but he understood that the primary way in which we become like Christ is through suffering.

The Russian novelist Aleksandr Solzhenitsyn spent much of his life in prison and labor camps, but he became a Christian while in exile. He wrote, "I turn back to the years of my imprisonment and say, sometimes to the astonishment of those about me, bless you prison. I nourished my soul there and I say without hesitation, bless you prison for having been in my life."

Paul would have said the same. It was suffering, after all, that made him more like his greatest treasure.

We're so afraid of hardship and suffering and rejection for the sake of Christ, but are we pushing away the means by which God intends to make us most like his Son?

—

Paul longs for us to be transformed, just as he longs for that himself.

"We eagerly awake a Savior ... the Lord Jesus Christ, who, by the power that

enables him to bring everything under his control, will transform our lowly bodies so that they will be like his glorious body." (Philippians 3:20-21)

He's talking about the last day, the day the Lord will return, when all sin and suffering will be swallowed up, when the dead in Christ will be resurrected to eternal life, and we will become perfectly like him because we will see him face to face.

In the Old Testament book of Exodus, even the leader of God's people, Moses, is granted only a glimpse of God's glory, and even then, it's only reflected glory. The result is that Moses' face is transformed. It becomes radiant, so much so that the people are afraid to come near him.

What will it be like for you and I on that day when we actually see the Lord Jesus face to face?

We'll be transformed, says Paul – and not just our faces, our entire bodies – so that they'll be like Jesus: gloriously free, without sin or shame or any taint of mortality.

—

If one day Jesus will make us perfectly like him, does that mean we should just take it easy in the meantime? Many of us treat the Christian life as little more than a waiting room for the next life: somewhere to wait passively until your number is called and you go to heaven.

For Paul, that's unthinkable. Christ is his joy, his treasure. He pictures himself as an athlete in a race, totally focused, straining every muscle toward the finish line when he'll finally see Christ face to face. He says:

"I press on to take hold of that for which Christ Jesus took hold of me ... one thing I do: Forgetting what is behind and straining toward what is ahead, I press on toward the goal to win the prize for which God has called me heavenward in Christ Jesus." (Philippians 3:12-14)

Is that the pattern of your Christian life too?

—

For many of us, forgetting what is behind is the hardest thing of all. My dad has a charcoal portrait of me as a kid. I'm nine years old. I'm on a fantastic family holiday in Paris. Everybody is having a great time. And I look miserable.

I think some of us just tend that way naturally. We're always trying to swim back upstream to the moment just before we think it all went wrong. Past conversations, past incidents, past relationships. What if I'd done things differently? What if I'd said something else? What if I'd been someone else? We pace up and down rehearsing and re-rehearsing dialogue as if we were preparing for opening night on Broadway, except of course there is no play. These conversations ended long ago. And many of the people who shared them with us are now long gone.

But if anyone had reason to feel regret, it was Paul. He was, in his own words, a blasphemer, a persecutor, and a violent man. Paul hounded Christian men and women from their homes, had them incarcerated, voted to have them killed, and approved the stoning of Stephen, one of the early church's most beloved and powerful leaders. Scripture goes so far as to say that Paul began to destroy the church. After all that, how can Paul say, *"Forgetting what is behind"* (Philippians 3:13)? How could he live with himself?

He could forget what was behind because he knew it was forgiven, all of it. He couldn't say, "I just can't forgive myself," because then he'd be saying that his own verdict on his past was more important than God's verdict on his past.

Hilda (Peru): Jesus helped me. Because in his word, in Romans, it says that we all have sinned, but he forgives us everything, and he doesn't remember my sins – so that makes me happy. I feel calm and at peace because of that.

Barry: That, I think, explains why Paul loves Christ so much. He loves him so much because Christ had forgiven him so much. Christ knew that Paul had tried to destroy his church, but Jesus allowed himself to be destroyed so that Paul could be forgiven. When you know you've been forgiven much, you love much. It transforms you.

I think back to how little I loved the people in my church as a younger man. I wonder if the reason I loved so little is because I thought that there was so little in me to forgive.

—

You know that Jesus gives you a better future. But do you know, if you're a Christian, that he also gives you a better past? Just think back over your history, no matter how checkered: all the things you did or did not do, all those choices made in cowardice or carelessness or foolishness, whether through oversight, ignorance, or malice. Paul knew that God had ordained all of those moments to make us more like Christ.

As the pastor John Newton used to say, "Everything is needful that he sends. Nothing is needful that he withholds."

Yes, if you had your time over again, you'd choose differently, but realize this: your Father, whose name is Love, would not.

Yes, if there is repenting to be done, repent – but then follow Paul's example, and look up to Christ. Take your place in wonder alongside Paul, the Philippians, and all the rest of God's people.

You've found the treasure, the pearl of great price. He's worth more than everything you've ever had, and everything you've ever lost.

And nothing in your past, present, or future separates you from him.

Episode 7: Rejoicing in Christ

[Philippians 4:1-9]

Barry: Here in the United States, every year there are approximately 19,000 major church conflicts. That's an average of nearly 50 a day, and those are just the significant ones, the ones that leave lasting scars.

1,500 pastors leave their post every month because of conflicts, burnouts, or moral failure. Four to eight million lawsuits are filed by professing Christians every year, often against other Christians, at a cost of between 20 and 40 billion dollars.

And that's just the visible financial costs. What about the largely invisible spiritual costs?

Lenny (USA): Man, lots of frustration, lots of anger, lots of tears, and probably lots of complaining to my wife. She's probably sick of me complaining about it.

It was an emotional roller-coaster because at the end of it, the only thing that was on my mind was the students, and I was like, "They've been through enough transition, youth pastor after youth pastor," and there was no stability because of the guys leaving all the time. And I wanted to be that stability.

But eventually I had to leave, because it just wasn't a healthy environment.

Barry: The Philippian church was just as vulnerable. There was conflict and disagreement, significant enough that Paul actually names names – two women called Euodia and Syntyche.

And these women weren't pretend Christians either. He says that they both *"contended at my side in the cause of the gospel"* and that both their names *"are in the book of life"* (Philippians 4:3).

Paul is tactful enough not to go into details, but it's serious because no conflict like this is ever truly private. It begins to affect the whole church. He pleads with them that they would be of the same mind in the Lord, and then he says, *"Rejoice in the Lord always"* (Philippians 4:4).

Now, if we're in conflict with someone, how can we possibly get to a place where we're *"of the same mind"* and rejoicing? Isn't that just massively unrealistic?

The key is in a small phrase Paul repeats across the New Testament some 216 times. Once you're aware of it, you start seeing it everywhere. Paul never uses the word "Christian" in any of his letters. Instead, he describes believers as being "in the Lord" or "in Christ." Why is it so vital for us to see ourselves in that way?

—

Imagine you're an orphan. You're poverty-stricken. You don't have any living relatives. You've been homeless all your life.

But then, one day, someone comes up to you on the street and hands you a letter. You open it up, and you see your name printed at the top. The letter invites you to a huge mansion in the countryside, and when you get there, a man tells you that you'd better sit down.

You've been adopted by the wealthiest and most generous man in the country, and he's signed over everything to you.

The castles are yours. The paintings are yours. The cars are yours. The thousands of square miles of beautiful forests and rivers. He's signed it all over to you.

He's also, of course, incredibly rich, and everything in his bank account is yours, too.

Not only that, but it begins to dawn on you that you're no longer an orphan. You have the father you've always longed for, but never knew.

Now, wouldn't that change the way you saw everything?

Wouldn't you see the world with new eyes? And wouldn't your view of yourself change too – your sense of identity, your roots, your potential, your security, your hope, your future?

It would feel like being reborn.

—

But that story is almost nothing compared to the true story of who you are now as a child of almighty God and a co-heir with Jesus Christ.

When Paul says you're "in Christ" or "in the Lord," it means all that is Christ's is yours. Your life is hidden in his.

So his identity is yours. When God looks at you, his eyes fill with the same love he has for Jesus. You are his precious child.

Christ's perfectly obedient life is yours.

His death and resurrection are yours. Paul says that you were *"crucified with Christ"* (Galatians 2:20), *"buried with him,"* and *"raised with Christ"* (Colossians 2:12). More than that, you are *"seated ... with him in the heavenly realms"* (Ephesians 2:6), even while you're still on earth.

His inheritance, too, is yours. Eternal glory in the new heaven and the new earth.

—

The reality that you're in Christ changes the way that you resist temptation too.

When you feel temptation biting, you can say, "No, that's not the person I am any more. I'm in Christ."

The early Christian theologian Augustine sinned sexually again and again in his early life – but then Christ changed everything for him.

This is a story I haven't been able to source, but the story goes that while walking in the street one day, he saw an old girlfriend walking toward him.

Augustine immediately went in the other direction, and she called after him, "Augustine, it is I!" "I know," he said, "but it is not I."

That's how we battle sin in our Christian lives. When temptation crashes over us, we say, "That's not who I am anymore. It is not I. I am in Christ."

—

And if we do sin, we don't plunge into despair – because we're in Christ, and our lives are hidden in his. We're covered by his perfect righteousness. So on the one hand, we're not complacent about sin – because we're in Christ. But on the other hand, we're not crushed when we do sin – because we're in Christ.

—

And there's something else. It's not just that you are in Christ. Christ is in you.

Paul says here, *"The Lord is near"* (Philippians 4:5). A reminder that his Spirit is in you, the Spirit of the one who calmed the storm, loved the lonely and marginalized, healed the sick, raised the dead to life. He is in you, and you're in him.

In other words, you're united in your innermost being with God himself.

Being in Christ is better than any other benefit the gospel gives us. Because everything else flows from it.

—

Can you see that Christian life is not about straining to be something you're not? It's about being who you are in Christ. When you do that, everything changes.

It changes the way you relate to God, the way you relate to yourself, and the way you relate to others. The way Euodia relates to Syntyche, and vice versa. Paul's saying to them, "Remember, both of you, that you're in Christ. You don't have to get your way. Have you forgotten? You've got it all. You're no longer orphans scrabbling around after the pennies of approval or power or recognition, so let your gentleness be evident to all."

This is why Paul says, *"Rejoice in the Lord always. I will say it again: Rejoice!"* (Philippians 4:4). How can we not stop fighting and rejoice when we remember who we are in the Lord.

—

And remember that phrase, *"The Lord is near."* As well as being a reminder that Christ's Spirit now lives in us, it's also a reminder that the Lord will return soon to judge all things.

I saw an Internet meme recently which said, "I'm not arguing. I'm just explaining why I'm right."

If I find myself in persistent conflict with someone, it might be because I want to vindicate myself. I want to show that I'm right, have everyone recognize that I'm right. I want to be the judge.

But Paul gives us a gentle reminder: there already is a Judge, and, unlike me, he's right 100% of the time. Christ alone knows who's truly guilty, and to what extent, and so that means we can leave the judging to him.

That doesn't mean we shouldn't be discerning, and concerned for justice. But it does take the heat out of so many personal disagreements if you can say to yourself, "Even if no one else recognizes what's going on here, there is someone who does, and he'll one day repay each person according to what they've done. So I can be gentle with others and rejoice."

—

I can also hear what Paul says next: *"Do not be anxious about anything"* (Philippians 4:6).

The key, if we want to resist anxiety, is *"in every situation, by prayer and petition, with thanksgiving, present your requests to God"* (Philippians 4:6).

Paul wants us to talk to God about anything and everything we're anxious about, knowing that our Father ordains everything for our ultimate good, and loves us as deeply as he loves his Son.

He tells us to pray, not just lists of things that we want, but with thanksgiving, thanking our Father for all he is. The result, says Paul, is that *"the peace of God, which transcends all understanding, will guard your hearts and your minds"* – here's that phrase again – *"in Christ Jesus"* (Philippians 4:7).

The way to be anxious about nothing is to be prayerful about everything.

Could there be a connection between how much we worry and how little we pray?

Lenny: I go back to the work that Jesus did on the cross, and how it talks about the veil in the temple that was torn – ripped in two. That literally means that we've got direct access to God the Father. No more priests on our behalf anymore.

Because of the work of Jesus Christ, we've got direct access. That Scripture ––"Come before the throne boldly" – that comes into play, and it's a beautiful thing.

What's beautiful for me is that he wants to talk with me. He wants me to come to him in prayer.

That's the difference between true Christianity and all these other religions. Religion is what you have to do to get close to your god or your deity. True Christianity is about God wanting to get close to us.

That's the whole reason why he put Jesus on the cross – to establish that relationship that Adam jacked up back in Genesis.

That's amazing to me that the Creator of all of this, the dude who said, "Let there be light," wants to sit in the presence of Lenny.

We do that whole thing: "God, I'm chasing after you." He's chasing after us! And he's like, "Hey, come on. I got stuff I want to show you. I got stuff I want to reveal to you."

Barry: Now, of course, we can't just empty our minds of anxiety. We have to displace it. We have to force it out. We have to fill the space with something else so the anxiety has no place to take root.

That's why Paul tells us:

"Whatever is true, whatever is noble, whatever is right, whatever is pure, whatever is lovely, whatever is admirable – if anything is excellent or praiseworthy – think about such things" (Philippians 4:8) – and that is a perfect description of Christ. Because everything that is most admirable, most excellent, and most praiseworthy is seen most fully in him.

Paul's saying, "Do whatever you can to fill your mind with Christ."

—

What might it do for your peace, your anxiety, your conflict with others, and your joy if, when you wake up tomorrow, you remind yourself of one single truth: "I am in Christ."

Episode 8: Content in Christ

Simo (Serbia): Before I became a Christian, I looked for contentment in films, cinemas.

Mostly cowboys. Oh, that was something special to me.

And also in drinking with my friends. We used to go to cinema with a bottle of whiskey in the pocket, and we were drinking and looking at the films.

That was my life. That was my contentment before I became a Christian.

[Philippians 4:10-23]

Barry: What do you need to be content? What is the one thing you feel you lack? And you think to yourself, "If I just had that, then I'd be happy. I could handle anything as long as I had that."

For a long time for me, it was marriage. I was single into my mid-forties, and the temptation was to think that everything I struggled with in life – times of depression, times of intense loneliness – all of that would be somehow fixed when I got married. My life would finally begin.

Now, my wife is an incredible woman, but can another human being really fulfill our deepest longings for lasting happiness and wholeness?

I think many of us believe that. We think that the secret of contentment is changing our present circumstances in some way. Get more approval, get more stuff, live in a nicer home, surround myself with people who love me more, understand me better, and then I'll be content.

But how much is enough? How much approval or power or comfort do we need before we finally feel content?

One poll asked Americans how much money they believed it would take them to realize the American dream. Americans who earned $25,000 a year believed it

would take $54,000 a year. Those who made $100,000 on average believed it would take $192,000.

Apparently our contentment requires about twice as much as we currently have – however much we currently have.

—

But as he signs off his letter to the Philippians, Paul turns all that upside down. He says that he's learned to be content whatever the circumstances, even apparently if you happen to be chained to a Roman guard, effectively on death row.

He sees that real contentment isn't anything to do with how much you have or how little. He says:

"I have learned the secret of being content in any and every situation, whether well fed or hungry, whether living in plenty or in want." (Philippians 4:12)

—

Now, I think I can make the case that Philippians chapter four verse 13 is the most abused verse in Scripture. It's usually translated, "I can do all things through him who gives me strength." It's the kind of thing athletes get tattooed on their biceps, as if it means they can run faster and jump higher if they're in Christ.

But a better translation is the one here. "I can do all this" – "this" meaning contentment in every situation – "through him who gives me strength."

You and I can have deep and lasting contentment, but it can only be found in Christ.

Now the Philippians seem to get this, that real contentment can only be found in Christ. You can tell that the Philippians aren't looking for contentment in money or material possessions, because they've been so generous with Paul.

Even though they were really young followers of Christ, Paul tells us here that they were the only church who supported him when he set out from Macedonia to plant other churches – sending him aid more than once when he was in need.

He describes it as sharing in his troubles. Not just sending money or a gift, but loving him so much that there's a deep emotional connection between them. It's as if his troubles are their troubles, and their troubles are his.

It's a lovely illustration of one of the main themes of Paul's letter: koinonia, partnership, togetherness. Not just pretending to care about others, but feeling their pain almost as if it's our own, and giving as generously to them as we'd give to ourselves. That's the kind of church Paul wants us to be creating.

Lenny (USA): There were nights where we were sitting on the couch watching TV. This one particular night, we were sitting on the couch watching TV – 9:00/10:00 at night. All of a sudden, there was a knock at the door. I'm like, "Who's knocking at the door this late at night?"

I open my curtains to see. All I see is a black shadow running up the street.

I'm like, what? I open the door – there's a humongous box of groceries and an envelope with $300 in it. We lost it. Thinking about it now, I'm getting emotional.

Barry: Did you ever find out?

Lenny: No. My wife posted it on *Facebook*. She says, "Thank you to whoever left this box of groceries for us, and it's truly a work of God because you got Lenny's favorite cereal." It was Cinnamon Toast Crunch.

Barry: Now, Paul is at pains to point out – he's not saying all this because he's looking for another gift. He says here, *"I have more than enough"* (Philippians 4:18).

The reason he's encouraging them in their giving is really surprising. He says, *"What I desire is that more be credited to your account"* (Philippians 4:17). He's more interested in the blessing they will gain by the act of giving than any benefit he might get from the gift itself.

Can you imagine how much we would give, how much we would sacrifice ourselves for others, if we saw things in that way too? If we really believed the Lord Jesus' words that it's more blessed to give than to receive.

Again, once we've understood how wealthy we are in Christ, we're free to give and give and give emotionally, physically, and financially – knowing, as Paul says, that *"God will meet all your needs according to the riches of his glory in Christ Jesus"* (Philippians 4:19). We do this, trusting in the promise that we'll receive from Christ much more than we've given.

—

Paul began his letter to the Philippians by reminding them of the one reality that changes everything: *"To all God's holy people **in Christ Jesus** at Philippi"* (Philippians 1:1). And now he ends the letter by reminding them of the same reality, *"Greet all of God's people **in Christ Jesus**"* (Philippians 4:21).

Because of that reality, Paul knows that the bond between them can't be stretched or broken by the small matter of a thousand miles. They're in Christ together. And that's as true today as it was then.

"The brothers and sisters who are with me send greetings. All God's people here send you greetings, especially those who belong to Caesar's household." (Philippians 4:21-22)

I wonder if there was a little twinkle in Paul's eye as he wrote that. There he was, chained to a Roman guard, and now even those in the highest courts of the Roman Empire are coming to know the grace of the Lord Jesus Christ for themselves.

—

We learn something profound about contentment from the Psalms in the Old Testament.

This is what King David wrote:

"I do not concern myself with great matters or things too wonderful for me. But I have calmed and quieted myself, I am like a weaned child with its mother; like a weaned child I am content." (Psalm 131:1-2)

Now, a weaned child is content simply being in his mother's arms. He's calm and quiet, because he's learned to trust his mother completely, even though of course a small child can't possibly understand what's going on in a parent's mind.

And it's the same with Paul. He's no longer anxious or fretful when things don't go the way he wants or expects. He's content in any and every situation, because it's enough just to be in the arms of Christ.

—

Basma: "I have learned to be content, whatever the circumstances."

Nashwan: "I know what it is to be in need…"

Antoine: "and I know what it is to have plenty."

Barbara: "I have learned the secret of being content…"

Rafael: "in any and every situation…"

Prasoon: "whether well fed or hungry…"

Lenny: "whether living in plenty or in want."

Simo: "I can do all this through Christ who gives me strength."

It's wonderful to serve Christ! It's so… I really… I'm just… feeling short of time.

Barry: So what is the secret of Paul's contentment? As I've read and re-read Philippians, I've started to see it on every page, and it can be your secret too.

Whatever your circumstances, whether rich or poor, single or married, in prison or free, even in depression and loneliness, the reality is that your Father is with you.

He's in the tears. He's in the hardship. And yes, he's in control. His fingerprints are all over your chains, whatever they may be.

Remember how God dashed Paul's plans and brought him to Philippi so that the Philippians could be saved? Remember how God made Paul's chains the very means by which the gospel reached the most powerful places on earth? Remember how God ordained that the cross, an instrument of torture, would become the instrument of salvation?

Barbara: When I gave birth, I had so much love for my boy. I felt like my heart was in him, and the first thing that came to mind is that, wow, God loves me this much.

And every time I look at him, even when he makes mistakes, the first thing that comes to mind is, "God loves you more than you actually love your son, and has much more in store for you than what you could do for your son."

Jesus says, "You are wicked, but you can give your children good things. How much more will God do for you?"

Barry: In my most troubled moments, as I think about what I've lost or what I've never had, yes, it's good to grieve. It's right to grieve.

But there's something Paul is saying to me in those moments: "Forget what is behind, remember who your Father is, and remember who you are."

I am in Christ. I'm unimaginably rich in him.

And even if the wheels have fallen off, I'm nearly home.

ACKNOWLEDGMENTS

Discipleship Explored Handbooks

Author	Barry Cooper
Editor	Alison Mitchell
Designer	André Parker

Discipleship Explored Films

Director	Stephen McCaskell
Producer	Stephen McCaskell
Director of Photography	Eric Skwarczynski
Assistant Director	Nate Morgan Locke
Screenplay	Barry Cooper
Teacher	Barry Cooper

Special Thanks

Rafael and Hilda Ahunari, Thabiti Anyabwile, Chris Arnold, Lenny Barber, Tracey Chang, Mark Dever, Don Elmore, Ivan Fawzi, Prasoon Goel, Dina Haddadin Hashweh, Tom Hough, Jem Hovil, Alberto Jaquez, Jonathan Leeman, Jeremy Marshall, Samantha McCaskell, Cat Morgan Locke, Simo Ralevic, Antoine Rutayisire, SAMAIR Peru, John Poon, Ian Roberts, Tara Skwarczynski, and Barbara Umuhoza

Dedicated To

Andrianna Lee Cooper, my Rib

SUPPORTING
WEBSITE

discipleship.explo.red is the official website for *Discipleship Explored*, featuring content for both guests and leaders.

Registering your course is free, and gives you access to even more content. You'll also be able to watch the films online and share them with others.

Christianity Explored Ministries (CEM) provides resources which explain the Christian faith clearly and relevantly from Scripture. CEM receives royalties from the sale of these resources, but is reliant on donations for the majority of its income. CEM is registered for charitable purposes in both the United Kingdom and the USA. **www.explo.red**

AVAILABLE FROM

CHRISTIANITY
EXPLORED
MINISTRIES

Leader's kits contain everything you need to get started.

For more information visit

www.explo.red

BIBLICAL | RELEVANT | ACCESSIBLE

At The Good Book Company, we are dedicated to helping Christians and local churches grow. We believe that God's growth process always starts with hearing clearly what he has said to us through his timeless word—the Bible.

Ever since we opened our doors in 1991, we have been striving to produce Bible-based resources that bring glory to God. We have grown to become an international provider of user-friendly resources to the Christian community, with believers of all backgrounds and denominations using our books, Bible studies, devotionals, evangelistic resources, and DVD-based courses.

We want to equip ordinary Christians to live for Christ day by day, and churches to grow in their knowledge of God, their love for one another, and the effectiveness of their outreach.

Call us for a discussion of your needs or visit one of our local websites for more information on the resources and services we provide.

Your friends at The Good Book Company

thegoodbook.com | thegoodbook.co.uk
thegoodbook.com.au | thegoodbook.co.nz
thegoodbook.co.in